In Search Of Ireland Again

John Butler

PNEUMA SPRINGS PUBLISHING UK

First Published in 2012 by:
Pneuma Springs Publishing

In Search Of Ireland Again
Copyright © 2012 In Search Of Ireland Again

Pneuma Springs

British Library Cataloguing in Publication Data

Butler, John.
  In search of Ireland again.
  1. Butler, John--Travel--Ireland. 2. Ireland--
  Description and travel. 3. Ireland--History. 4. Ireland--
  Social conditions. 5. Morton, H. V. (Henry Vollam),
  1892-1979. In search of Ireland.
  I. Title
  914.1'5'0483-dc23

  ISBN-13: 9781907728389

Pneuma Springs Publishing
A Subsidiary of Pneuma Springs Ltd.
7 Groveherst Road, Dartford Kent, DA1 5JD.
E: admin@pneumasprings.co.uk
W: www.pneumasprings.co.uk

Acknowledgement

The extracts from In Search of Ireland by H V Morton at pages 19, 33, 54,
57, 59, 67, 83, 107-8, 118, 122-3, 133, 134, 147
are reproduced by permission of Methuen Publishing Limited.

Photograph of 'The Claddagh, Galway' by courtesy of Independent
Newspapers Limited, Dublin
Photograph of 'Fair Day' by courtesy of Stan Mason

Disclaimer
Photograph of 'Cinderella in Connemara' – Unfortunately, I have not
been able to trace the copyright owner. If anyone knows them, please
inform me.

Contents

Chapter VIII
I revel at the scenery to Ballyshannon, note the empty beaches, make comparisons caused by EEU. No sign of recession.

Chapter IX
I am told all about St.Patrick, hear about Croag Patrick and the pilgrims, see Clew Bay and am told the story of Grace O'Malley.

Chapter X
Sligo and W.B.Yeats. Note the sparse fields. We are in Celtic Ireland, find my grandmother came from Mayo, hear about the links with the Ormondes. I pass through Ballina and halt at Crossmalina, meet Michael— to Bangor, remember the words of HVM. Out at sea is Achill, a sense of auld Ireland, I am bemused at Claggan.

Chapter XI
I read of Thomas Jefferson of Wymondam, think of a Jefferson who became President of the U.S.A., wonder if there is a connection.

Chapter XII
Achill Island, centre of Celtic Ireland. I think of the hard life they led, the annual migration to the mainland for work. I note the changes through the years, see the pre Irish beehive huts, here the past meets today.

Chapter XIII
At Newport I find Grace Kelly's birthplace, then on to Knock, once again, I am bemused. It is the 130th anniversary of the 'sightings'. At Westport I buy some tobacco and hear about 'the priests'. I hear about 'the haemorrhage' and the mass migration. I am saddened.

Chapter XIV
I remember Cong from the film 'The Quiet Man' with John Wayne. It is still living off its memories. I see the procession to Sunday Mass. Clifden has not altered over the last twenty years, it stands, looking out over the Atlantic to America. The real capital of Connemara is Boston, Massachusetts. I learn of the history of Connemara. I hear of the Tuatha De Danaan people. I feel the magic of Connemara.

Chapter XV
I meet two friends who run Gregg Castle. I join an Irish Folk Dance group, meet a knowledgeable pair from Tipperary - come to Galway, compare it

with the past, tell of my excitement to see 'the Claddagh'. Learn about 'Lynch Law'. Find the home of James Joyce, hear Bing sing:
'To see the moonlight o'er the Claddagh
And watch the sun go down
O'er Galway Bay.'

Chapter XVI
HMV writes of the scene eighty years ago – no railways, shops, cars, telegraph poles, no sound of donkeys' hooves on rocky soil. I hear the word 'poteen', learn how HVM got it. The changes over the years.

Chapter XVII
Celtic Ireland and Connemara, Alcock and Brown, Kylemore Abbey, its sad history. Marconi and the first radio message to Nova Scotia

Chapter XVIII
To Limerick, its siege and history. Irish Town and English Town, the Protestant Ascendency. England's shame.

Chapter XIX
I find Tipperary disappointing, once the largest barrack town in the UK. Now deserted. Shabby shops, dreary weather. I wonder at the nostalgia of the old army song.

Chapter XX
On the way to Killarny. I stay to marvel at the 'cosmetic' beauty of Adare. I sense the ghost of HVM as we near the lakes; recall his boatmen and their tales, mix with the throngs of tourists. I am entranced by the lakes. I am told of strange people that once lived in the valley. Kerry and its early spring, in summer the botanist's paradise. I marvel at the beauties of Muckross and move on to the Dingle.

Chapter XXI
The spectacular road of mountains, sea and woodland, the land of the 'small' farmer. The Shannon Power Scheme and the electrification of Ireland. The film Ryan's Daughter and its impact. I come to Tralee and its festival.

Chapter XXII
I visit Macroom and think of Spike Milligan. The beauty of Glengariff and its links with the Royals and the famous. I hear of William Penn and Pennsylvania.

Chapter XXXIV
Rocky road to Dublin. Recall meeting the Mayor in 1947 – Uncle Barney and the Gaiety Theatre. Book of Kells. The three cathedrals. I visit the Guinness Factory and compare changes over the years. O'Connell Street and Nelson's Column. Recall 1916 rebellion. St Michan's – shake hands with a crusader. Spiders.

Chapter XXXV
On to Drogheda. Hear about the siege. Remind a lady that Cromwell is dead.

Chapter XXXVI
Newgrange, older than Stonehenge. Its association with time. Tara residence of the High Kings 2000 years before Christianity.

Chapter XXXVII
At Dundalk think of John McCormack. Learn the meaning of 'beyond the pale'

Chapter XXXVIII
Dundalk and the changes

Chapter XXXIX
N1 to Newry, reach Warren Point. IRA bombing. Connections with the Brontes, Wuthering Heights and Heathcliffe. Compare Carlingford with 20 years ago, 'the troubles'

Chapter XL
Cross the border. Compare with 1992, armed forces. Come to Rahfriland – Patrick Bronte's school

Chapter XLI
Armagh, Irish Canterbury. Again make comparisons. Theme Park.

Chapter XLII
Carrickfergus Castle, Paul Jones, William Congreave, Jonathan Swift, Louis MacNeice, Andrew Jackson and the President of the U.S.A.

Chapter XLIII
Belfast, Ballynahinch and Humanity Martin. Ranjit Singhi. Newtownards –

busy manufacturing town. Scrabo Park, the Ark. I see the film 'Mutiny on the Bounty' starring Franchot Tone descendant of Wolfe Tone.

Chapter XLIV
Ulster provided half the Presidents of the U.S.A. I reach Larne on the last stage of my journey.

Extra Information –
More about Ireland (At a Glance)
Bibliography
Index

Introduction

I have long been a disciple of that King of travel-writers, HV Morton. His most treasured epistle, the one that forever lives in my memory, is his 'In Search of Ireland'. He came to Ireland eighty years ago. My first visit was in 1947 followed by a tour in 1992. Now, in 2009, I am eager to see how Ireland, the home of my ancestors, has dealt with the changes. So when the opportunity arose, I set off, many years after the master, to follow in his footsteps, and my own earlier ones.

Circumstances obliged me to follow his trail in reverse, but still covering the same places.

Accordingly then I set off for Stranraer to take the ferry to Larne.

I

Scotland, before devolution, was already a different country from England; you felt it the moment you crossed the border. The country may be geographically joined to England and our histories entwined but the villages and cottages were as different from England as any village in France or Germany. I had come to the border across the Cheviots and the magnificent Carter Bar and now as I stood with my back to England, facing Scotland with its heather clad purple hills rolling away before me, I felt the sadness of the centuries of blight and disruption that had afflicted this beautiful country. At the same time I became aware of a large middle-aged lady standing beside me. She was sobbing silently into her handkerchief and I heard her murmur, in a strong Australian accent;

'I've come back Mum; to let you see it again, as you always wanted to but never made it.'

I was touched and felt an immediate empathy with her, even though I have no Scottish blood.

I came into Newton Stewart on a dry sunny day. The town was a bright contrast to last night, when, in a downpour it presented a most depressing appearance. Now the streets are throng with people and with its bustling little shops and cafes it looks alive and attractive. What a difference the weather makes!

By 10 am I was on my way to Stranraer through the lovely, enchanting countryside of the border. The Highlands may be best known but there is equal beauty, if not grandeur in the borderlands. I felt tempted to linger but my quest is Ireland and Scotland must take its turn for a future venture.

Stranraer seemed a pleasant little place and a busy port to boot.

Seeing as I had a few hours to spare, Castle St. John, (a 16th century stone keep that had been used for various purposes, including a prison, and was now a museum), seemed as pleasant a place as any to pass the time.

The museum presented an historical survey of Stranraer through the centuries. Its wax figures in their period costumes brought it startlingly to life.

The ferry left at 3.45pm. The passage was smooth and uneventful but at the first sight of land I felt an inward surge of anticipation at seeing again, after so many years, the land of my forefathers. It was a fine, if somewhat boisterous day, weather-wise as I stood in the prow looking anxiously for the first sighting of land; my Ireland!

I was joined by a native returning home to Ulster. He was of indeterminate political persuasion and seemed reluctant to commit himself to any hard and fast political conclusion. He professed a cynical but firm view that the troubles were all about money and economics. I had timidly put forward a fair and balanced opinion as to the merits of both sides but his Irish fluency with the English language bedazzled me and I began to wonder if perhaps, he was right! Our dialogue was cut short as we both, simultaneously, sighted land. We stood there, dumb, as the little green strip of land on the horizon drew nearer, ever nearer.

II

It is sad that this little island that holds such nostalgic memories for so many millions all over the world, for so many generations of exiles, cannot find peace among its own sparsely populated peoples. The burning question now, in 2009, is will the peace last?

However, my quest will be strictly A- Political. I am anxious to see how the island has changed over the years.

I was quickly out of Larne and on the A2 North -coast road, and what an introduction to Ireland it is! The road really does run beside the coast and what splendid scenes unfurl as it winds its way up north. It was an added blessing that the coast road was so quiet that lovely August evening; there is so much to distract one. Every curve and bend in the winding road brings fresh bursts of delight as scene after scene of unrivalled beauty unfurls itself before my eyes.

The coast road northwards to the Giant's Causeway is truly magnificent in the golden glow of the evening. The claim that it is as fine, if not finer than the Corniche Road in the south of France, seems borne out.

The hills lie backward to the left for the whole of the eighty miles; while on the right lies the clear blue sea, where at its closest point, a mere twelve miles distant, is Scotland, in the shape of Rathlin Island where Robert the Bruce had his meeting with the Spider. We are told that its tireless efforts inspired him to return and defeat the English at Bannockburn. That was in 1314 but we are in Ireland now and it may well have been last week.

On this clear August evening one could pick out Islay and the Paps of Jura, while over the low Mull of Kintyre one could see the head of Goatfell and the mountains of Arran. This is truly a memorable journey.

Inevitably, as the evening advanced, the necessity to find a place to rest arose. I had no intention of planning even one day ahead as far as bodily needs were concerned. I was on an adventure, a disciplined one but not a regimented one, to follow in the footsteps of the Master.

I was so entranced by the beauty of the coast road, the peacefulness of the dying day and above all, the indefinable feeling of warmth and contentment, that I felt it almost a shame to have the practicalities of living intrude.

I settled at last for a little village on the coast by the name of Glenarm. The long main street of the village was full of parked cars, lined on both sides of the road. Apart from them, the village showed no signs of life. In contrast to the idyllic scene I had just left, there seemed here to hang an awful air of anti-climax. Once again I was dragged back to those awful years of suffering that this beautiful part of the world had endured. Gazing down the silent, empty street, something of that tragedy was transmitted to me.

My spirits were not raised when a form of human life exhibited itself in the shape of a small gang of youths, dressed as most youths of today in the indistinguishable, classless, and shabby, dirty, jeans, scruffy trainers and obligatory black bomber jacket. What did distinguish them from their 'look-alikes' in England, was their mien. In England, such a gathering, while looking alike as two peas in a pod, would have been alive, noisy and giving off a general air of energy and potential aggressiveness. Here, there seemed among them, a pathetic air of hopelessness and lethargy. Maybe it was all in the mind. Perhaps I was unable to dismiss the pre-conception 'we' across the water have had forced upon us over the long terrible years. Be that as it may, it had a sobering effect on my elated spirits. Nor was I in any way relieved when two hundred yards further on, I saw, huddled in a doorway, a group of young girls, seemingly as dour as the boys, sitting silently, waiting, hoping, for I know not what. The fact that both groups seemed oblivious of each other, only helped to deepen my gloom.

Although I was unable to find even one place in Glenarm to dine, I did find a place to rest -'Margaret's Guest House', a quaint 18th/19th century cottage that had been converted into a B&B. Inside, Dolly Varden would have felt at home. Nothing seemed to have changed since that era. There was nothing quaint about the hostess. However, she was warm, friendly and full of Irish hospitality...but no evening meal! On her advice I drove up the coast road again for two miles until I came upon a small fishing port called Carnlough. In comparison to Glenarm it was a Metropolis! A grey walled harbour held a few fishing boats and on the sea front were one or two decent looking little hotels and a few small shops - bravely open to the last. Behind them stretched a collection of neat terrace houses, all with a car parked outside. Behind them rose a range of steep hills, green purple and brown heathered, with a forest of young trees climbing up their slopes. There was however, a sense of quiet sadness about the place. I suspected my feelings were not yet objective and I resolved to fight this shadow of the past and see things as they really are...today – 2009.

I found a café, if that is the right word, (it is what the sign outside said.) At home, in Yorkshire, it would have been called a 'fish and chip' shop, with a few chairs and tables inside for those customers who did not want to walk the streets eating their meal.

Due to the fact the evening had decided to turn nippy, I opted to dine inside. The food was good. The service, well intended but sporadic: the bread and butter, a long time after the meal, the ice-cream even longer and the tea...forgotten!

At a nearby table sat a man and woman, who, I would guess were in their early thirties. They seemed to be having some kind of trouble with the proprietress. They were from Germany and did not realise that Ulster was still part of the UK and Sterling was still our currency. It was 10pm and outside, dark and chilly. I felt a sudden weariness creep over me. It had been a long but interesting day. I made my way back to Glenarm and 'Margaret's'.

III

Thursday 9am.
Margaret's Guest House - wrapped in a time capsule of the 1920's/30's; much like Mr. Straw's House in Worksop. The house itself was much older: 18th or early 19th century, I should guess. Glenarm is one of the oldest villages on the coast road. There are the remains of a castle on the way out and in 1992, the Police Station, like all the Police Stations in Northern Ireland, is sealed up; the place itself resembles a fort with a barbed wire compound.

In 2009, things look better!

The road from Glenarm to Ballymena runs through delightful countryside. I had hoped to see the little white cabins that HVMorton encountered but alas, they have gone.
In their place are large, expensive looking houses and bungalows, all picked out in brilliant white. Most of them were built in the seventies and eighties of this century. Not as romantic looking as the traditional cabins but no doubt decidedly more comfortable to live in.

I was interested as to how this housing 'revolution' had come about. The government, I was told, had subsidised these dwellings on condition they were made available for B&B tourism.
I passed through the little township of Drummore. Its wide main street was packed with cars, nose to tail. A war memorial, seen only in Ulster, never in the Republic, along with numerous shops and houses was proudly flying the Union Flag.

The road led through Ballymena, meaning 'middle village', a comparatively large, bustling place with its narrow streets choc-a-bloc with traffic. On the surface, there seems little sign of a recession. Some years ago, Ballymena was named as the centre for the renamed 'Irish Regiment' that was formed from the merger of the 'Irish Rangers' and

'Irish Brigade'. This, I thought, must surely have made it a target for the I.R.A.

The road continues through the delightful countryside. It is undulating with rich farm-lands either side. Again, I looked, in vain, for any sign of the traditional Irish cabin with its turf roof and whitewashed walls, like the Hollywood movies and, who knows…perhaps John Wayne with his arm round Maureen O' Hara standing in the doorway. Alas, it is now only history…

IV

Ulster is proud of its nine glens, arguably, the most beautiful being Glen Ariff.

Glen Ariff: gateway to Fairyland!

Was ever such natural beauty encompassed together in this exotic spot? As one proceeds down the Glen, with all the beauty that nature can crowd into its two miles, there are high, purple mountains on either side and at certain points, a view of the towering coastal headland with the vast expanse of the Irish Sea stretching away to the horizon.

I come across two fast -flowing streams merging and tumbling over brown, glistening rocks. The rushing water is multi-coloured; brown, gold and shining silver; a stream of fairy gold!

Everywhere, the foliage is thick and luxuriant. The sound of falling water can be heard, like fairy bells, long before it can be seen. If there are fairies in Ireland, they must surely live here.

Reluctantly I bid farewell to this magical place and head for Cushendall, a heavenly little spot beside the sea, and then on to the quaint, picturesque little port of Cushendun. This was created by Clough Ellis, perhaps more memorable for Portmeirion, in Wales and even more so for the TV serial, 'Danger Man' that was made there. The mountainous coast road to Ballycastle is unbelievably beautiful; at every turn there are breath-taking views of cliffs, sea and hills.

There is such an air of peace and prosperity about that it is hard to imagine the troubles that this beautiful part of the world has suffered over the last forty years.

Ballycastle itself, is a small commercialised sea-side town, busy and thriving. The beach has unrivalled sands but alas, is almost deserted. It is never warm enough for bathing. Near the harbour is a memorial to Marconi, whose assistant sent the first wireless message across the water from here to Rathlin Island in 1898.

There was little reason to dally further so I pushed on to my next stop - Ballintoy. A steep path leads to a sharp chasm in the cliffs. Here the Carrick-a-Rede Rope Bridge leads 65 feet across an expanse of water, bubbling and foaming over sharp rocks a hundred feet below to the salmon fishery on the tiny island. Here in 2009 tourists are queuing up to pay £4 a time to venture across it. I recalled H.V. Morton's description, all those years ago. He described it as:

"the nastiest bridge you will find anywhere. It is made of two parallel ropes, with cross ropes, on which planks are laid. There is a rope handrail which swings about in the wind. In fact the whole bridge sways in a most alarming manner. Below is a drop of about a hundred feet to sharp rocks."

That was written eighty years ago. In 1992 it had not altered and hundreds of tourists, myself included, 'dared' to cross the perilous chasm. It was fun. The bridge is still there but since the National Trust bought the site, they have considerably reduced its precariousness. This new footbridge is much stronger, less dangerous and not as thrilling! To make it sway today requires the effort of many tugging it. A lot safer but less fun! Streams of people still trudge the mile long path on the cliff edge, just for the thrill of crossing this 'dangerous' bridge. Truly, a human phenomenon! It is not an entertainment; it still has its potential dangers (although nothing like the old one.)

The Giant's Causeway is only a few miles up the coast. On the way is a bay called, 'Port o' Spain'. Here a great Spanish Galleon, fleeing from the defeat of the Armada in 1588, was wrecked in a terrific storm. All were lost, including, Admiral Alonzo de Layhe. The wreck has only recently been found and its remains can be seen in the museum in Belfast.

V

It is getting late and since I have not pre -booked any place, I decide to make for Portrush and return to the Giant's Causeway tomorrow. When I arrive it is dark, cold and raining. I am not inspired.

9 a.m. The morning is bright and dry. The sun is not yet shining over the headland to the south although the sky shows promising signs. The sea is as still and flat as a steel mirror. Portrush looks more attractive in the day than after dark.

It is a typical 'working class' seaside holiday resort with the usual cheap shops, restaurants and places of entertainment. The wide crescent shaped beach is beautiful with its sparklingly clear sand but it is deserted except for two small boys playing football.

Portrush is built on a promontory that thrusts itself out for nearly a mile into the Atlantic and could have been designed by nature as a perfect holiday resort. Alas, the vagaries of the weather in this part of the world are not part of its attraction.
The Mecca for so many of the world's visitors is the Giant's Causeway, arbitrarily at times, called one of the seven wonders of the world but derided by others as an over-photographed celebrity, now lies before me in real life. The main road runs some miles from the cliff-face and it is necessary to turn off down the lane that leads to the complex of car-parks, cafes, shops and museum. The Heritage Centre that one meets before taking the long trail down the cliff, boasts a video film that gives a complete historical and geological account of this unique rock formation.

I will confess on first seeing The Causeway, I was somewhat disappointed; so less grand than the portraits and photographs. I felt in agreement with Dr. Johnson who was asked: "worth seeing?"
"Yes".
"Worth coming all this way to see?"

"No!"

I can sympathise with his statement when one thinks of the effort to get here in those days.

Thackeray said, on arriving here:

"To think I've travelled 150 miles to see this!"

It is interesting to remember that it is only since 1740 that any real notice has been taken of the Giant's Causeway. An obscure young lady painter from Dublin made some spectacular sketches of it and aroused public interest. It became an attraction overnight and when the railways came, trips from Belfast were very popular. Local guides offered their services and besides giving tourists the factual geological details also related the folk-tale of Finn McCool, a great Irish giant who built the causeway so that he could reach Scotland to fight another giant who lived in Fingal's Cave. The guides were steeped in these legends.

The geological facts may not be so romantic to the layman tourist but to the geologist they are equally so.

There are three divisions of this geological freak: the Little Causeway, the Middle and the Grand Causeway. There are over 40,000 quite separate vertical columns of rock. From the distance they look like a cubist presentation. There is something inexpressibly weird about these thousands of seemingly, mathematically formed pillars which thrust themselves upward at the edge of the sea. The overall impression is one of a metallic grey, resembling iron or steel. The rock formations in the cliff-face are equally strange.

There is a strange mathematical exactitude of the Causeway that impresses one. The vertical columns are all separate but set so closely together that it seems a knife-blade could not be thrust between them. Most of them are six -sided, but others have five or seven sides. Oddly, it is said, there are only three nine-sided columns in the 40,000 and only one three sided. A guide pointed out an octagon, a pentagon and a hexagon, all together. There is a 'Wishing Chair' which is formed by columns that rise to ten feet or so with a little platform on which is a comfortable, natural seat, with a back and two arms. Then there is 'The Ladies Fan', a marvellous arrangement of five perfect pentagons sunk around a heptagon. It was a thrill, to see in life, this Irish natural wonder which shares with the Blarney Stone in the south, the distinction of being the only feature of Ireland which is well known by the rest of the world.

The cliff path back looked long, high and tiring but an alternative route led straight up the cliff face. There were over a hundred steps. I toiled silently along behind two elderly, well built, gentlemen, who turned out to be German tourists. At the top, one turned to me and said: "Good exercise?... Yes?"

It had been arduous I agreed and the rest was much appreciated. While they were recovering, they spoke to me. One had been an officer in the German army, the Wermacht. He went to great lengths to explain he was never in the S.S. The Wermacht, he confessed, had a hearty dislike of them. He said how necessary it was for him to keep in touch with the English language. He was well educated and we had an interesting conversation about the similarity between the English and the German languages. He spoke admiringly of the word, 'window'; 'the eye of the wind'. Although English is now a polyglot language, borrowing from many others, he spoke of the common Anglo-Saxon links and the German background of the Royal family. He confessed that his visit to Northern Ireland was due to the news coverage of the 'troubles'. He thought the newspapers had sensationalised the events and he was agreeably surprised at the seemingly normality of life here. They both expressed firm ideas on how 'they' would have dealt with terrorists!

It was now getting late in the afternoon and time I moved on. I followed the coast road and around 6pm arrived at Londonderry. I dined, very adequately, at Gilhooley's Wine Bar on delicious fresh mussels, baked hot bread and a glass of the incomparable Bulmer's Cider. In Ireland, it has perforce to be called Bulmer's. It is manufactured by Bulmers but because there is an English Bulmers, also manufacturing cider, the name, 'Magners' has been adopted for the Irish version when sold in England.

The stroll into town did not take long; and at 8.30 pm, with the sinking sun hanging just above the Cathedral, reflecting its golden rays on the city walls and its surrounding river, it presented a spectacular sight.

There are only two cities in England to compare with Derry; they are York and Chester. Like its English cousins, its walls are complete and like the others, Old Derry has broken its ancient confines and now spreads beyond the walls on every side. The walls are about twenty five feet high and well preserved.

The history of Derry is both dramatic and heroic. The feuding between Celt and Saxon is long and bloody but it was deepened during Tudor and Reformation times. Rebellion after rebellion was crushed by Elizabeth. The lands were taken from the native Irish and waves of settlers, 'English undertakers', as they became known, undertook to live in Ireland and 'Anglicize' it.

They were followed by thousands of Scots; still known as the 'Ulster Scots'. Sir Walter Raleigh alone, received 42,000 acres, while Spenser received Kilcolman Castle, County Cork. It was while he was here, from 1586 to 1590 that he wrote the 'Faerie Queene.'

VI

August 2009
Tomorrow is the Apprentice Boys' Parade with its procession of Marching Bands; 14,000 strong.
After all the years of trouble I was curious, while still uneasy, to see it again.

I recalled all those years ago when I last visited Derry. It was 1992, 'The Troubles' were still on.
I remember seeing, when crossing the bridge, the number of armed R.U.C. men, carrying out a check on all vehicles entering and leaving the city. I asked if this was because of 'The Apprentice Boys' march. He said it was a normal routine check.
As I entered the town, I was dismayed to see everything shuttered, dead and silent, as if waiting to die. It was the lull before the storm!

Near the Court House, then an army barracks, a huge Check-Point Tower had been built; it looked menacing and formidable. Walking as casual as I thought appropriate, I passed, unchallenged into a large Protestant, 'working class' estate of council houses, called 'The Fountain'. Litter was everywhere; the first I had seen in Northern Ireland. The place was deserted and a quiet menace seemed to hang over it. Here and there, the Union Jack and the Ulster flag bravely fluttered. On the waste ground below the city walls and adjoining the council estate, several youths were practising drumming for the great parade, next day. A gigantic bonfire was heaped high and on top was the Republican flag, ready to burn.

Then, the noise began! What a noise! Drums. Seemingly thousands of them, all being attacked with tremendous fervour and vigour.

A native must have noticed the alarm on my face, for he stopped me and with a friendly smile assured me it was only 'the boys', practising their drumming. If this was only practising, what would the real thing be like? I began to sense the fear, if I were a Catholic, in this community.

By 9.30 am the next day, Saturday, crowds were already moving into the city and finding places along the route to be taken by the Marching Bands.

At that time in the morning, the R.U.C. with their flak jackets, revolvers and machine guns seemed to almost outnumber the civilian population. Here and there you could spy a British soldier, rifle at the ready, alert for any trouble.

I stood alongside a young soldier. He was from Essex. I asked him how long he had been here.
"Fifteen months," he replied.
"Have you seen much action?"
He laughed,
"No. I'm bored to death."
I was surprised, to say the least.

A little further on, I came across a R.U.C. man, leaning casually over a barrier, rifle with telescopic sight, held ready to pick anyone out acting suspiciously. It was all so natural that I was amazed I accepted it so easily.

Like most Irishman, he liked to talk. He was very knowledgeable about 'the Troubles'. Like others, he thought the Press were responsible for much of the 'hype' and it gave a much distorted picture of the situation in Northern Ireland.
"Not that there hasn't been any trouble," he hastily added, "but there has been more disturbance on the mainland than Derry."

I had walked in from Waterside, where I had found accommodation. This was in 1992. It was now a strong Protestant area. As one stoical Protestant put it...
"We were bombed out!"

25

Londonderry, or Derry, as they call it, is an unpretentious city. There is a war memorial in 'The Diamond', the city centre.

Another RUC man I spoke to agreed with me, and to the world outside, that the whole thing appeared ridiculous but it went a long way back and was now a fact. Now, it was a case of 'tit for tat' and both sides were out for revenge. And thus it goes on. Londonderry, he said, was now a divided city. There had been bombings of Protestant business men's homes, necessitating their removal to Waterside.

That Saturday in 1992, it was a warm, sunny day, for which I was thankful, for it was a long wait for the 'Marches' to start.

There had been a service in the Cathedral which made me ponder still further what all this feuding between Catholic and Protestant was about. But then, as the Irishman on the boat emphasised,
"It's not religion; it's money!"

Crowds of men, in their best Sunday suits, carrying rolled umbrellas and wearing old fashioned bowler hats poured in from two directions and joined up outside the Cathedral. Round their necks was proudly displayed, their Lodge Sashes.
The first detachment came marching up the hill to the Diamond at about 12.30pm. The groups were all in the same formation - a line of side-drums, followed by a huge drum which a burly drummer beat with almost savage ferocity.

This drummer was accompanied by two very small boys, either side of him, who clashed their cymbals almost as energetically. Behind these two front lines were the pipers, or the flutes, or sometimes, bagpipes and accordions. The sound was ear-splitting!

Each group wore a different uniform. They marched very proudly, followed by the men in civilian attire, with their bowler hats and rolled umbrellas. Flanking them, were men, right arm extended in front of them, carrying upright, gleaming sabres.
Leading every group was a small boy with a Drum-Major's baton. They competed with each other as to who could do the most dexterous manipulations: twisting, turning, throwing them high in the air.

Each group carried its own branch banner of the 'Derry Boy Apprentices'. Along with all this were the Ulster flags and the Union Jack. I found it very moving to watch this show of loyalty to their country and the UK and even more ear-splitting to listen to.

Although there was a kind of carnival atmosphere, there was also a grim seriousness about it too. A statement was being made! These people will never give way to Republican pressure for a united Ireland! It is difficult for foreigners to understand that these parades have been going on since the Siege of Derry was lifted in 1689.

I estimate that there must have been 20,000 or more in the parade. It took three to four hours to pass by. Even though there was no disturbance from the Catholic Derryites, the presence of armoured cars in every street, was disturbing.

After it was over, the litter was unbelievable. Fast-food stalls had lined the streets wherever the procession went. The scene was devastation! I was plunged from a sense of pride and emotion to one of despair. The cold realities of life!

All that was nearly twenty years ago but so seared into my mind as if it were yesterday.

I watched the parades again today–2009. They were still spectacular and moving but the military presence was not obvious and all went without incident.

The Siege of Derry and the Battle of the Boyne has always struck me as rather bizarre affairs. From the coverage that H.V. Morton gives them, I am inclined to think he thought so too.
To the ordinary 'man in the street', in England it was plain Catholic v Protestant but when you hear that Protestant William had the blessing of the Pope, the issue becomes confused. We have to go back to Tudor times to help us unravel it.

Sir Walter Raleigh, along with Humphrey Gilbert and Spenser, saw Northern Ireland as a place where fortunes could be made, personal services rendered to the Queen and the true cause of Protestantism could be upheld against Catholicism. All of them were stone blind as to the realities of the Irish racial and religious problems. The abolition of the Irish upper class to make room for English Landlords began under the Tudors and completed under Cromwell, left the peasant nation with no leaders but the Parish Priests. (It is only recently that an Irishman admitted to me his relief that 'the power of the priests' had at last been broken.)

When Catholic King James came to the throne, all Ireland with the exception of Protestant Ulster supported him. Although James's priority was security of the English crown, he nevertheless had no intention of neglecting his claims to Ireland. With French assistance an army was raised and he invaded at Kinsale in March 1688. The Protestants declared for William and thousands of refugees poured into the walled city of Derry.

James was now in a bit of a dilemma. His pro-Catholic sympathies had led him to appoint fellow Catholics to key positions in England. This was not popular with the English Protestants whose support he needed nor also with the English Catholics themselves.

The Irish Catholics forced him to summon Parliament. The Catholic Irish Landlords were restored to their land by the repeal of The Act of Settlement and nearly all the Protestant landowners lost their property. James now lost their support.

A few weeks later, James marched on Derry. The Governor wanted to surrender but the people decided to defend the city.

James had no siege guns so he decided he would starve the city into surrender. A boom was built across the Foyle to prevent supplies being sent in but toward the end of July the boom was broken and two ships, the Phoenix and the Mountjoy reached the city with ample supplies. Derry had survived 105 days of siege, during which the people had been reduced to eating cats, dogs, rats and mice.

A visitor to Derry cannot escape being told of the 'Apprentice Boys' who gallantly closed the city gates against the besieging army.

I noticed that nearly every time I called the city, Londonderry, I would be gently but firmly told 'they' called it Derry.

I was interested to know how the prefix London came about. It appears the Corporation of London was approached by the Lords of the Privy

Council with the suggestion that the rich City Companies might care to acquire land in Ulster. James had declared that four million acres of land, previously owned by the Earls was not their property but belonged to the clansmen. That was irrelevant to James and he pressed forward for a solid Protestant colony in the North. The land was described thus:

'The country is well watered by springs, brooks and rivers, plenty of fuel either by wood or turf. If fields are necessary for men's sustenance they are in such measures as may not only maintain steady but also furnish the City of London yearly with manifold provisions especially for the fleets, namely with beef, pork, fish, rye, peas and beans. It is fit for all sorts of husbandry.'

The screed goes on in further detail, almost eulogising over this little paradise, begging for investment. It is plain to see why the prefix, London, was added.

Another strange thing strikes me about this time of conflict in Northern Ireland, ostensibly between Protestant and Catholic. Few Catholics seem to know, or acknowledge, that the Pope not only knew but approved of the Protestant Armada. Innocent X1 had himself urged all Catholics to resist the French Jesuits and the Gallican Church.

So, when William set sail from Hellevoetsluis on a November day in 1688, he took with him, paradoxically, the blessings of the Holy See and the united hopes of Protestant Europe.

It was then, with mixed and heightened feelings, I left Londonderry, knowing that a few miles further and I would be leaving the UK and entering the Republic of Ireland.

You cannot miss Dunluce; it is an extraordinary castle, perched picturesquely on a rock high above the sea. It is often ignored because of its proximity to the Giant's Causeway. It is now a ruin, comparable to King Arthur's Tintagel. It has a banshee in the tower but it has not been heard lately.

The Border

When HV Morton arrived here in the Thirties, The 'Free-State' was then in its infancy. The Customs Officers searched his car for contraband.

Finding him 'clean', they took him into a tin hut to settle the other issue. The new law was that if you take a car into the Free-State, as it was then known, you had to deposit a third of its value with the customs and similarly if you took it out into Ulster.

Twenty years ago, it was much easier. There was a military checkpoint and beyond that a small custom shed that was the border. It was empty and entry into the Republic was open.

Now, in 2009, it is even more casual.

And so I came to Letterkenny; an interesting looking little town, quite prosperous it seemed. It has a huge hospital. I am in Donegal and while the countryside is attractive the roads are quite atrocious!

Further down the A56 is Dunfanaghy, a tiny village on the Northern coast of Donegal. It hasn't changed. It is as quaint and well maintained as it was twenty years ago. The private houses were still outstandingly attractive. A pleasant place to live, indeed.

It is Sunday and the churches are full. I drove up to the Headland. There are huge sweeps of empty sands, bays and islands. There are mountains all around and in the distance. The Atlantic Ocean spreads emptily to New York and America.

I met two English people - a lady from Warwick, who had lived in N. Ireland for fifty years and her husband from Ware. They now live in Drummagh near Derry and love the South of Ireland and Donegal.

There is a scenic route to Donegal which I found as bumpy and twisty, as it was years ago but it hugs the coast all the way. The views are still spectacular. What amazes me is the almost continual string of houses, pubs, cafes, snack-bars and petrol stations. Perhaps 'string' is not the right word. These are what are called villages in Ireland. They are nothing like the traditional English village where the community is grouped round the church, the village green or town square. Here a village can stretch for miles with no central focal point; just houses, sprinkled everywhere over the hillsides. Here and there you see an occasional street with a few shops on the main road. Nothing much has changed over the years.

As I said, what I did find amazing in 1992 were the dwellings themselves. I expected, and hoped to see the traditional white, turf-roofed cottages of old Ireland. Instead I found immaculate houses and bungalows. The size of some was staggering.
They are still here; sparklingly white with every modern convenience. They differ only in size and opulence.

In the HV Morton tour, the 'cabins' were a characteristic of Ireland…they were Ireland! Where had they gone? Twenty years ago they were sparse; now they are extinct. The only place you will find them is in the splendid Theme Parks and Museums.

All these new dwellings appeared to offer B&B. I found accommodation in a five bedroomed bungalow, set well back from the roadside. It may well have been the same one I stayed in before in 1992.
It was run very efficiently by an elderly couple. Pat, as he insisted I call him, had been a farmer on this land for many years. He was born in a 'cabin' (the ruins of which I could just see, buried in a small jungle of brush and tangle way behind us) but when the Government of the Republic offered him a huge subsidy to build this bungalow on condition it was used for tourist purposes when necessary, he jumped at the opportunity.
He doesn't farm now. The B&B, besides providing a nice little earner, also gave him another life.
"We get folk from all over the world," he said. "I love it!"
This obviously applied to all the other houses and bungalows.

In the surrounding fields are piles of peat, drying. There is a huge peat bog here. Now and then, one passes a very modern looking snack-bar, exactly like any other in GB or America. It destroys the illusion of the old West of Ireland but as tourism has grown so huge, these come too, to meet its needs.

As the road winds its way over the picturesque countryside, one sees great houses in extensive grounds. Some are still in private hands while others have become high class hotels.

VII

The road to the county town of Donegal runs downhill for many miles. The approach to the town is pleasant. The little church stands on the banks of the Eske and a stone bridge leads to the town centre, the Diamond.

The town itself, I remember, as twenty years ago, was most disappointing. On that Sunday evening it was throng with people and traffic. They were mainly young men and women dressed in the usual attire. The place looked as if it had been invaded by a horde of wild savages. Add to that the litter that was everywhere, the line upon line of parked cars, the endless stream of traffic that was threading its way through the cluttered, busy streets, the unwholesome appearance of the shops and you have a fair impression of Donegal town on a Sunday evening in August, in 1992.
It was not unlike an English town comparable in size, on a Sunday night.

Even down at the head of the lough, a pretty area, there was an air of neglect. All this contrasted strongly with some of the substantial houses and bungalows on the outskirts. The little restaurants, cafes and pubs, all looked grubby and uninviting, but they were full of people, again, mostly youngsters. It was as if the older residents of the town had taken refuge, this Sunday evening.

Donegal, in 1992 was a disappointment. Donegal, to me, had such an Irish ring about it that I wonder now, with hindsight, whether I had anticipated too much.

There is no doubt that Ireland has benefited tremendously from its union with Europe but when you think that in the not too distant past, its population was double what it is today...?
Emigration is still a problem. Ireland cannot keep its young.

Long ago, when HV Morton visited Donegal, it was raining. He was told,
"When it's not raining, it looks like rain."

The scene was very different then:
'In the wide square in the town centre, a few drovers stood with long sticks, while a few cattle stood about and blundered on the pavement. Now and then, carts laden with turf and vegetables set off, through the drizzle down the road.'

I suspect he must have had the same misgivings as me, because he writes:
'Ireland is full of towns whose names have gone round the world with a kind of splendour to them so that the stranger, expecting towers and turrets and great crowds comes instead with a kind of wonder to a little town like Donegal, where men huddle in the drizzle and a few calves low sadly on the pavement'.

It is only when we realise that the fame of these places is borne by the home-sickness and nostalgia of emigrants, that the disappointment is overcome.

Donegal has certainly changed since then but the disappointment remains.

VIII

It is fourteen miles from Donegal to Ballyshannon and the road to the left has steep hills littered with sparse grass covered boulders that rise steeply to mountains weathered in misty clouds that suddenly dissolve in a burst of bright sunshine and transfigure the whole countryside. To the right is the Atlantic Ocean. The beaches are unbelievable; nowhere in the world are there such gloriously clean, firm, golden sands. The day is fine, warm and calm and the little white waves throw themselves on to these pathetically empty beaches. If only Ireland had the summer temperatures of Spain! But then, it would perhaps be a pity to see such a lovely countryside and beaches desecrated, as they would be, if ever they became popular with the outside world. But the rest of the world is cut off from the West of Ireland!

Many years ago, before the 2nd World War, until Ireland joined the Common Market, this part of the country was a poverty-stricken isolated back-water, hardly civilized. Little white turf-roofed cabins were sprinkled over the land in as much disorder as a handful of stars. It is all gone now! Here and there one might catch a glimpse of a ruin that was once home to a family.

Today, scattered all over the hillside or set well back from the road, are expensive looking houses and bungalows.

I was told the places were not expensive to build, or at least, buy. They were almost identical in design, if not in size. £35,000 I was informed was the average. The same in England would be £150,000, I estimate. They are built on the large concrete block system and the walls insulated with foam. They are then painted a brilliant white. They are now numerous and spread out, sprawling from village to village and all displaying the B&B sign!

The European Economic Union has been very generous towards the small Irish farmer and he has known undreamed of prosperity since joining the Common Market.

Ballyshannon seemed much bigger and more interesting than Donegal. (It wasn't raining.) All the houses, including some fine old Georgian ones and the old terrace houses lining the streets, were immaculate and well-cared for. The shops were well-stocked and quite busy. Unemployment in Ireland is 10% but there is no appearance of such.

IX

St. Patrick.
There is something about the Irish that is different. When a saying or a situation crops up that is not quite straightforward, we are tempted to say:-
"That sounds a bit Irish."

St. Patrick, the patron saint of Ireland, whose name is revered by all Irishmen the world over and whose face and form, are everywhere displayed in this island, was not even an Irishman!
Most stories tell that Patrick, a Welshman was kidnapped by pirates and brought to Ireland. He was a shepherd, and then went to France to study Christianity. He returned to Ireland in 432 as a missionary, although not the first. In 431, the Pope, Celestine, had already sent Palladius.

The story goes on how in 439 AD, Patrick retired to a great mountain in Connaught to commune with God. For forty days he fasted there, we are told, with much weeping, wailing, (it omits gnashing of teeth, although he probably did that as well.)
It is said that while he was here he banished all snakes from Ireland.

Croagh Patrick, or in English, Patrick's Hill rises over 2000 feet over Clew Bay. There is a chapel at the top and this is a Mecca for thousands of pilgrims from all over the world and especially from the U.S.A.

It is Ireland's Holy Mountain and many of the more devout remove their shoes and stockings and take the hard path barefoot.

From Clew Bay you can see, lying out perhaps four miles from the land, a small green island called Clare Island. On the shore, facing the mainland is the ruined tower of Grace O' Malley's Castle.

Grace O' Malley is as well known in Ireland as Rob Roy in Scotland and her name comes up in songs and legends of old Ireland. She lived in Tudor times; she was a female pirate. She was the daughter of Owen O' Malley, a pirate who dominated the seaboard of Connaght. She lived in an age of piracy, the age of Francis Drake. She was declared an outlaw by the English Government and a huge reward offered for her capture. When her husband died, she married a powerful Anglo-Norman called Sir Richard Bourke but after twelve months she ended their union.

This remarkable woman, then, in 1576, went to Galway and offered Sir Henry Sidney her fleet of three galleys and 200 men in service of the Queen. This startling alliance led, in 1593, to her being invited to London and the Royal Court.

Grace is buried in Clare Abbey. A gruesome story is then told that in the nineteenth century a company was formed in Scotland for the acquisition of bones for manure. A ship was fitted out which raided the West of Ireland where immense quantities of bones were piled up in churchyards and old abbeys. Grace's bones, we are told, most likely went to manure some Scottish acres!

X

Sligo is another twenty three miles further down the coast road. The tiny farms, both arable and grazing, are unlike any in England. Here are little stone-walled enclosed pockets of brown earth on which a few potatoes are grown. Adjoining them is a green patch of root crops. All around is the thick heather and sparse pasture where a cow or two will be grazing. The one or two acre plots are criss-crossed with dry stone walls. However, making a living now is easier than it ever was before The Common Market.

On entering Sligo, one thinks of the Irish poet, William Butler Yeats. This is where he spent much of his youth and the influence it had on his work. He loved it and he is buried in the little church-yard at Drumcliffe. One of his most famous poems is, 'Under Ben Bulben.'
The flat-topped mountain, in the afternoon sunlight, cast a shadow down its side, giving it the appearance of wearing a dark cloak.

The town was larger and busier than I had imagined it. Everywhere there were cars, the streets were alive with them.
They were parked on both sides, in effect, virtually making it a one lane passage.
There are bookshops by the score and, as one might expect, the works of W.B.Yeats are prominently displayed. The bustle and noise here is almost unbearable; it takes the pleasure out of it.
However, for anyone seeking Celtic Ireland, its heritage and folklore this is it! The cultural heartland of the Northwest, lies in and around Sligo, the only sizeable town in the region from where you can reach several prehistoric remains and other historic sights.

I knew that my paternal grandmother, Margaret McHale, came from Mayo. I was surprised to find it is not an uncommon name in these parts. She married a Butler from Kilkenny and when I met her, they were

Landlords of a Public House, in Westminster, called 'The Duke of Ormonde'. Considering the Butlers were the Dukes of Ormonde I thought it was perhaps more than a coincidence. I shall never know.

Passing through Ballina I called a halt at Crossmalina, a tiny picturesque little Irish town. In the centre of the town is a monument to the Virgin Mary.

Once again, the traffic was heavy and did nothing to enhance the place. Everywhere-right, left and centre, were cars; parked on either side of the road or streaming endlessly through the congested narrow streets.

There are a lot of Michaels in Ireland. (Remember the Michael in the film, 'Ryan's Daughter'...the village idiot?) One came up to me as I was about to take a shot of the village. He was a tiny, fragile looking young man in his mid twenties. His clothes were a mere collection of 'hand-downs' of all sizes and shapes that looked as though they had been thrown at him. But it was his demeanor that struck one. His pale, thin white face bore an expression of such benign imbecility; grinning from ear to ear, that it was impossible not to feel moved. He strutted past me like a young cockerel and stood, chest out, erect and beaming. I obligingly took his photograph. He obviously thought he was doing me a great favour, for he bowed and marched briskly away.

On to Bangor, (very different from the Welsh one!) with its modern Marina, down the coast to Mulrany. I am still trying to follow the route of HVM but many years later, things have changed. It is this change I find fascinating.

The surrounding countryside however seems unchanged. As I stood on the hill overlooking the sea, perhaps in the very steps of HVM, I recalled his words as he watched the setting sun sink below the Atlantic Ocean. He wrote:
'An unearthly beauty pulsates in the air; it is an opalescence which seems to have a music in it'.

Standing here on this warm August evening I feel the very essence of his words.

Beyond, rising out of the sea, are the blue mountains of Achill. Over Clew Bay can be seen Croagh Patrick and beyond are the Twelve Pins and the wild 'Joyce' country.

I stayed the night at one of the modern bungalows overlooking Clew Bay and Achill Island. It could have been any bungalow in the British Isles. It was clean, warm and homely. I had some 'real' Irish stew for supper!

I am trying to write as I continue the trail but before I finish for today, I feel I must record an experience I had at Claggan that stirred my emotions.

XI

Claggan is no more! Whatever it was...village, hamlet or just one of a scattered community, it has gone!

Standing in complete isolation is a tiny church: roofless, windowless, as empty inside as a skeleton. Even the floor - mere trodden earth, covered with a blanket of nettles, malignant looking weeds and sheep-droppings. Close by this sorrowful scene was an old grave-stone. I could still discern the epitaph on it. It read:

'Here lies Thomas Jefferson of Wymondham in Norfolk, who died at Claggan in 1868.'

This was the only visible grave left in the tiny churchyard. All around, there is nothing but a collection of nettle and weed covered mounds. Horned sheep roam freely, almost like guardians of the place. It is more than depressing. There lies over it a sense of sorrow and loss that at times becomes overwhelming.

Through a gap in the surrounding hedge lies the large Manse, Rectory or Vicarage. It stands alone, forlorn, empty except for a chair and table in the living room. The presence of these two articles of furniture seemed to deepen the sadness of this once homely, peaceful residence. The long driveway to the house and the once spacious lawn is now a forest of giant, man-high nettles, thistles and bracken that one has to literally fight one's way through.

It is here, the church and house, were the centre of a community. Now a pile of bricks and mortar.

Where is it now? I pondered on the name, Jefferson, then I thought of Wymondham, in Norfolk and Abraham Lincoln. His family came from that area. Jefferson was another American President that may also have had roots in Norfolk. Ireland is a predominantly Catholic country but I don't think this incumbent was Catholic. I would guess Wesleyan Methodist but I have not been able to trace any further.

XII

Achill Island is still, probably, the most Irish part of Ireland left before it is swallowed up in the great European Union.

When HVM made his tour, seven thousand people lived on Achill Island. What struck him most was the Irishness of the island. In his words:
'They speak in Irish and they think in Irish'
He wrote of how beautiful and colourful the place was when it was fine but how, in stormy weather, with:
'the wind tearing round the mountains like forty thousand devils and the wild Atlantic waves screaming at them from every side, battering their pitiful little stone cabins, some clustered incredibly on stone ledges jutting out into the sea.'
What a hard life! And yet, here he found a people who loved dancing and singing, and the constant sound of their fiddles, (like the twittering of sparrows) and poverty, the like of which he had never seen before!

In the spring, every able-bodied man and often young woman, left Achill for the mainland of England or Scotland where they would labour for the next five months, on farms or wherever they could earn money to pay their debts, back home.

This was the pattern of their lives, with special boats from Glasgow or Liverpool arriving to collect them. Generation after generation knew no other life than this. The women who were left behind had to work their little potato patches themselves and strive until their men returned in the autumn. It made them prematurely old; old at thirty, senile at forty, bent and wrinkled so that their age defied recognition.
Such was the Achill Island in the 1930s!

Now, tourism and entry into the European community has changed all that. Apart from the ruins of the old cabins, and stone 'beehive' huts still clustered over the hillsides, there is no sign of any great poverty. Modern bungalows, all catering for the tourist trade, have replaced them.

These beehive huts, compared to which, the cabins seem almost grand, are reminders of an Ireland older than the Irish.

It is with mixed feelings that now one can find accommodation in a modern bungalow with central heating and look out onto the still wild countryside and think of the hard life these islanders led but still loved. This is Ireland; linked to the present, eager for the future but always in the past.

XIII

Newport is a small one street town, busy with a constant stream of traffic threading its way past the line of double parked cars. There were three things I noted:
a) Grace Kelly was born here; her cottage can still be viewed.
b) The R.C. Church has one of the most beautiful stained glass windows, anywhere in the world; well worth a visit by itself.
c) In 1798 a contingent of the French army, in support of the Irish rebellion that year, attempted a landing here. The local parish priest supported them and for this he was hanged in the main street. There were huge posters in the town commemorating this abortive invasion. It was 1798 but again, this is Ireland, it could have been last week.

I kept on the main road until a B road pointed to Knock. I have many Catholic friends and have heard so much about it and its emergence as a national shrine after the 'apparitions' that I was more than a little eager to finally see for myself what it was like.
I hardly expected another 'Lourdes' but in Ireland one can never rule out anything.
I suppose everyone that comes here knows the story. This week is the 130th anniversary of the 'sightings' or 'Holy Visitations' as they are now called.

In 1879 Knock was a tiny village, typical of so many in Ireland. The people were poor farmers or labourers, Nothing had changed over the centuries. Life was bleak and uneventful and hard.

A farmer or farm labourer and his wife were returning home after a long, hard day in the fields. As they passed the village church the evening shadows cast by the sinking sun fell on the wall of the church and formed silhouettes of two shadowy figures; which the couple interpreted as Joseph and Mary. Others were summoned to see this 'miracle' and it is from this that Knock became famous the world over.

The Pope would not give it his approval but nevertheless, Knock has now become an international 'religious site' and has grown into its present 'monstrosity'. As a non-Catholic I can only see the multitude of shops selling religious bric-a-brac as sheer commercialism out of control. Knock now has an airport and large hotels.

It is impossible for me to express my feelings as I stand and stare at the crowds shuffling past the gable end wall of the church, prayer-beads in hand, heads bowed in reverence, and muttering their 'Hail Marys'. While it would be easy to express ridicule or sarcasm, I cannot but feel respect but at the same time, wonder, even envy that such faith can prevail today.
Again, this is Ireland...it is unique and I love it.

It is only a week since the crossing from Stranraer to Larne; it seems ages.

Leaving Knock, in still somewhat of a whirl, I headed North to Westport. I passed through numerous little villages, all with alluring names. Westport is a most attractive place. The Mall is a pleasant tree-lined road running alongside the river. There are two main streets that run parallel with each other and are lined with small individual shops, each one, a treasure trove in itself. All is bustle and buzz; an air of quiet prosperity and peace is prevalent... I like it!

Called in at one of these 'treasure caves' for an ounce of my favourite tobacco. I was served by a most stunning young woman whose radiant features were only surpassed by a head of   autumn gold hair that fell down her back in a cascade of waves. Such beauty is rarely seen. I thought to myself:
'Some young fellow is going to be lucky.'

There was something else, of a quite different nature that left me in surprise, if not shock. On display, quite openly, were packets of condoms. Modesty prevented me from making any comment to the girl but outside, in the street, I spoke to a Garda, (male of course) and told him of my surprise and shock, compared to twenty years ago.

45

He smiled and replied:
"Yes, thank God. At last we've broke the power of the Priests! They don't have the power and control over us like they did."
I nodded my assent but could not resist posing the question, "How do you reconcile birth-control with your religious faith about sexual relations?"
He smiled again.
"Ireland has to move with the times."

I would have liked to continue our discussion which I knew would eventually lead to the 'abortion' issue but I could sense that he too feared that and he excused himself and moved on. I find it sad that so many Catholics feel themselves restrained to freely discuss aspects of their faith. Maybe that is the difference between 'faith' and logic. I don't know.

Ballinrobe sounded attractive as so many of these quasi-villages do but unfortunately it ends there.
Ireland must be getting on to be half the size of England and has only a population of three to four million; similar to England in Tudor times. When you compare this to the present population of England (excluding Scotland and Wales) which is over 50,000,000, you realise what an empty country this is. Take away Dublin, Cork, Limerick and what are you left with? Hundreds of little towns and villages, many unchanged over the years and you have the perfect 'tourist' island.

Ireland's 'eternal haemorrhage' of its people, continues and will never end. There is nothing here to compare with the lure of New York and London for the ambitious young Irishman and woman. It is a sad but true fact.

XIV

I am looking forward to seeing Cong: two reasons. Firstly, a good friend of mine was born here and his stories of the hard life he had in an orphanage here, seemed very much in contrast with such a pretty little village. Then, of course this is where the film, 'The Quiet Man' was made with John Wayne and Victor McClaggan. Although it is many years since this quiet backwater experienced all the glamour of Hollywood it is still siphoning it off with signs marking where scenes were shot.
The cottage he shared with Maureen O Hara is at Clifden.

It was Sunday in Cong and in the evening it became throng with cars coming in for Mass. I stood and watched the car park fill up then overflow to the streets. It was a warm August evening and everything seemed right with the world. As the cars slowly filtered past me I could not fail to be impressed with the demeanour of their occupants. Never have I seen such pleasant, contented looking faces. If they were coming to some great exclusive concert, their faces could not have radiated such contentment. I envied them!

Clifden has not altered much since my last visit nearly twenty years ago. It has one main wide street built on a hill that slopes down to an estuary that points straight over the Atlantic to America. It is the capital of Connemara but as HV Morton pointed out:
'the real capital of Connemara is Boston, Massachusetts.'
That is probably not as true today as it was when he made it. America is still the goal of many Irishmen and women but not as much as in the 1930s. The Common Market and European Union has changed all that.

Long before I ever came to Ireland I would, in my imagination, see myself stood on a cliff edge, with the wind roaring in from the vast Atlantic Ocean with its three thousand miles of open sea to America, tearing round me, while I stared transfixed at the great foaming white horses of the waves, in a never ending fury crashing themselves furiously at the cruel rocks below me. And now, here I was, just as I had imagined... except for the weather.

It is a calm, mild August evening: the wind is not raging, nor are the waves like angry white horses, but the Atlantic is still there; three thousand miles of it and so is the magic of Connemara.

It must have held somewhat of the same spell over HVM for you feel the intensity of his emotions as he writes of this place as:
'Where the world ends!'

There were few roads and strangers seldom visited this area. The people of Connemara lived there much as their ancestors had done over the centuries. They were poor and had little class division.

HV Morton described it as a place that had been locked away for centuries by geography and poverty.
He declared that entering Connemara gave him a sense of discovery almost akin to the finding of Tutankhamen's tomb.
He was clearly overwhelmed by it!

Connemara is still wild and ruggedly beautiful. The wild Irish girls have gone; instead we have equally lively young ladies serving behind the modern bars and cafés. The white cabins have been replaced by modern bungalows, all serving B&B but the unique atmosphere remains. Ireland is a magical place! It has its fairies, its leprechauns, its ogres, its banshees and hosts of others from the spirit world but it is here in Connemara that is the most haunted.

In the centre of some of the fields is a raised piece of ground with a thorn bush on its summit. The farmer has left this alone and uncultivated. They call this a 'fort' or 'rath'. Legend has it they were built by the Danes. Others say it is a corrupted form of De Danann, the mysterious people called Tuatha De Danann ... the tribes of the Goddess Danu. They are said to have conquered Ireland by virtue of a great magic, but the Druids of the people of Mil were too strong for them; and magic meeting magic, Tuathade Danann were forced to fly and take refuge in the fairy mounds.

Every countryman in the west of Ireland knows that these places are haunted and are inviolable ...fairyland!

As I continue. To Galway, I cannot help but wonder at the state of the countryside. Comparisons, they say, are 'odious'. That may be true, of course, but one makes them nevertheless. For mile after mile, these leafy lanes are bordered by seemingly, neglected fields of grass. The lack of arable cultivation is striking. Even the dairy farms are small and the herds of cows even smaller: sometimes, no more than half a dozen. The farmhouse today is a modern, fair-sized bungalow that caters for B&B, perhaps not as a side-line but as the main source of income. In the fields adjacent to it, a few sheep graze. The farmer tells me he is paid for this state of things by order of the Common-Market economy philosophy. He doesn't grumble. It is much better than his forebears' hard life.

Every so often one sees an old ruin of a cabin; door bricked up, roofless, in a general state of decay. These cabins, once spread in their hundreds over the hillsides have gone! In their place, at intervals of only fifty or a hundred yards are the modern bungalows and houses, looking very grand and inviting. Connemara is now a tourist paradise, set in the past with its feet in the present.

XV

Gregg Castle, is now an hotel, run by two friends of mine. It was built in 1648 and its walls are ten feet thick. From the outside it looks very dour and grim. Inside, I was welcomed warmly and given the best bedroom: it is large and airy, too airy: draughts everywhere! The facilities are rather primitive too but the views are fine, sweeping over the wild surrounding countryside.

I am lucky! Wednesday night is the Irish Folk Dancing meeting.
The Great Hall is full of dancers, fiddlers are fiddling furiously, the Irish 'jig' is 'jigging' equally so. The place is alive with noise and human activity, a flurry of black-stockinged ladies legs and perspiring men, throwing themselves into the dance with energy and exuberance that more than makes up for any lack of skill or finesse. One cannot help but feel drawn into it like a magnet. Before I know it, I am in this mad whirlpool. No one notices or cares for this mad, solitary figure doing a whirling dervish solo in their midst. Tonight I am Irish and loving it.

The next morning is grey and forbidding. By 9a.m. rain is falling fast. I make my way to the dining hall. The twenty feet long table has still a few places left. Everyone is talking. Once again, contrasts. Its English counterpart ...silence!

The couple beside me are from Tipperary; they surprise me with their knowledge of British politics. Ireland has had its independence a good few years now but listening here, they still seem bound up, pretty much as before.

As I near Galway the countryside slides into a flat, unexciting vista but Galway itself looks as though it might be interesting.
It is busy, as it was twenty years ago. The old streets are narrow and crowded with people of all nationalities. This fact soon becomes obvious as you hear the foreign accents of Poland, Germany and France, all

around you. The shops, I was still delighted to find, had not lost their individuality since I was last here. All of them have Irish names. There is a big multiple ... Dunnes, on the outskirts.

HV Morton, on his visit commented on how Galway reflected Spain, with its square house with a central court-yard and a gate flush with the street. Galway has a long association with Spain. In the Middle Ages, it was the Bristol of Ireland with its quays packed with the wine casks of Spain. The Galleons of Galway were as accustomed to the ports of Spain as they were to Irish ports.

Galway, eighty years ago, had a population of only 14,000. A century before that it boasted 40,000! Today it is once more a thriving cosmopolitan town.

For many years, Galway was known as 'The Curse of Cromwell'. HV Morton called it 'the town of yesterday' He found it a town of dead factories and great houses brought into decay.

Galway, says HVMorton was known as Galway of the Tribes. The fourteen families that founded it became the most exclusive in Ireland.

During the Civil War, Galway remained loyal to the crown and Cromwell made them pay for it!

Irish humour is always there, even when it is deprecating. They tell a tale of the First World War:
A German submarine surfaced and prepared to shell Galway. A young officer made a reconnaissance first. He came back with the report that the town had already been bombed!

It is very different today. It is a cosmopolitan town; there are people of all nationalities here now. It is becoming a centre of culture with students of all nationalities.

An old Spanish type house, now a Bank, was once 'Lynch House'. There is a story to it:

In 1493, John Lynch Fitzstephen, Mayor of Galway, went over to Spain to improve trade relations. He was entertained by a rich merchant called Gomez, whose son, a handsome young Spaniard, returned to Ireland as his guest. Lynch had a son named Walter and the two men became friends. Walter was in love with a girl called Agnes, whose father, a merchant in Galway spoke Spanish perfectly. He welcomed the young Spaniard to his house. Walter Lynch became jealous and in his passion stabbed the young Spaniard and threw his body into the sea.

Walter was arrested and confessed his guilt. As Mayor, his father had to pronounce his death sentence. But no man would carry out the execution. The crowd, whose sympathies were with Walter, tried to surge forward to rescue him but Lynch stalled them by hanging his own son. This has now become known as 'Lynch Law' although it is exactly opposite to that.

The name, Nora Barnacle, may not be well known but at 8 Bowling Green, just round the corner from St. Nicholas' Church, is a house that was once the home of the wife of James Joyce, the famous novelist. Inside, it is a small museum with Joycean memorabilia and copies of letters they wrote to each other.

Twenty years ago, when I was in Galway, I was all agog to see 'the Claddagh'. I had heard so much about it, and Bing Crosby had made it famous with his song.

'To see the moonlight o'er the Claddagh,
And watch the sun go down o'er Galway Bay.'

I remember the impression it made upon HV Morton when he first saw it. He called it the most remarkable sight in Europe!

The Claddagh was a fishing village, long before Galway grew up beside it. Until 1954 it had its own king, its own laws, customs and costume and a thriving economy based on fishing. Their vessels were known as the 'Galway Hookers' and are today used for pleasure trips.

The Claddagh Ring is a ring with two hands, the symbol of friendship, holding a heart, the symbol of love.

Up to 1937, the Claddagh was a fishing village of neat, white-washed, thatched cottages planted at haphazard angles with no regular roads running through them. If you took three hundred little toy cottages and jumbled them up on a nursery floor, you would have something like the Claddagh. If a giant had spread a handful of peppercorn, it could not have been less organised.

I couldn't wait to see this wonderful spectacle and I pushed through the crowded streets until I came to the Claddagh. I could not believe my eyes! Before me was a housing estate such as one might find anywhere in England. Prim, neat, council houses, no doubt much preferable to live in than the white cabins of old. A solitary sign on a lamp-post informed this was 'The Claddagh'. Disappointment was not adequate, to say the least. An old man sitting on the quay side, sympathised with me, adding: 'they could have left a few'.

Another man was photographing a little stone monument.
It read: '...Christopher Columbus - sailor, who from these shores, realised there was land further west across the Atlantic'.
Puzzle, what does it mean?

An ancient citizen of Galway told me that when Galway was known as the city of the tribes, the native Irish had to live outside the city walls. They formed this little town of their own. There was a 'King of the Claddagh' who administered their own unwritten law.

To go further back than H V Morton, a Mr. Stephen Gwynn, in 1909, wrote:
'We have here the descendants, not of Spain but of that older Irish race who built the great dun of Aran...the Firbolg, whom the taller, stronger Milesian breed drove back into the mountains and islands. When one sees fair hair in this community, it is such as one finds in the south.
Mr. Gwynn goes on to give us this glimpse of the Claddagh, a hundred years ago:
I had to go through the whole village, house by house and it was odd enough at three and four in the afternoon to find strong young men rising up between the blankets in a corner of the little house. That of course is natural in a fishing community whose work is done at night.

But a thing struck me which I have never seen anywhere else in Ireland, where generally men have a prejudice against handling babies or doing anything that they think is a woman's work. But here, in at least a dozen houses, I found the woman bustling about while the man stood or sat with the infant in his arms and holding it as a woman does. It was curious to see and perhaps natural enough, for the women must be out, hawking their fresh fish at the street corners. It stamped on my mind that feeling of distinctiveness and aloofness in the Claddagh and its people. I have never found any community in Ireland, so shy, so alien, and so hard to know.'

HVMorton tells us. He walked through the Claddagh, late one afternoon. The fishermen were out and he saw only, very old men, standing at the corners, smoking their pipes. He says, 'there was one, he could have stepped from a Spanish galleon. There was nothing of the Firbolg about him. He was pure Spanish: tall, thin, sallow, long-headed, with fierce dark eyes, a pointed beard and in either ear a thin gold ring.'

The Claddagh was picturesque but it had attracted the attention of the sanitary authorities. The little cabins were pulled down and in their place came the modern council house.

In the old days the Claddagh never married outside itself. Now that's over and a Claddagh girl will marry a Galway boy.

It is at night, the Claddagh was most beautiful. There were no street lamps, no pavements, only open earth beaten hard by the feet of generations. The only light came through the open doors and windows. And the smell! Maybe the authorities had a point when the issue of sanitation heralded the end of the Claddagh.
But what was lost too was the all pervading distinctive aroma of the hundreds of peat fires belching their perfume over all.

I can't leave Galway without commenting on a Mass I attended in the town.
The Franciscan Abbey Church is a large grey-stoned columned building, looking more like a museum or an important bank.

Inside, it is surprisingly large and spacious. Down each centre aisle are white fluted, pilaster covered columns. The walls of the nave are covered in a pale pink wash, as is the high rounded roof. The huge white columned altar is set against a red background. High up in the wall is a large multi-coloured stained glass window. The overall effect is quite hideous. The church was packed with seated, silent people. They were joined by a continuous stream of newcomers who genuflected before seating themselves. The silence is overwhelming. It is as though we are all sitting …waiting, though for what, I know not! Although I am not a Roman Catholic, my background is what is referred to as 'High Church' (Anglo-Catholic), I attended out of sheer curiosity, I regret to say.

The Mass was long and tedious. 'Audience Participation' I should rate as two to nil. I may have entirely misjudged it but the spiritual atmosphere seemed to me, quite absent. It was like:
'We are here! That's enough!!'
Of course I may be entirely wrong. I suspect I am.

We are all waiting for the priest. Suddenly, a bell rings. The congregation rises and a priest, clothed in green garments, enters. He stands before the altar, raises his arms in an enfolding gesture…chants, (what seems to me) some meaningless mumbo-jumbo, to which the masses reply robot-like. It is difficult not to be disturbed by such a display of mass indoctrination but I recognise the affinity of the ritual with the High Church of the Anglo-Catholics.

I notice an abundance of fair-haired people who look very 'Anglo' and remember that many of Cromwell's men stayed here after it was conquered.
But for me, at least, there was one highlight. It may have nothing to do with the religion but it relieved the monotony of seeing the priest keep vanishing into, 'God knows where', having a swig of something then returning to administer some 'hands on' to a never-ending stream of humanity.

In front of me was a family of man, wife, and five or six children. The one that attracted my attention was a girl of about twelve, who was clearly bored out of her mind. She somehow felt a relief from this by every now and then, at regular intervals, flicking the elastic in her knickers. Surprisingly, this loud 'twang' went unnoticed or ignored throughout the proceedings, except for me who kept waiting anxiously for the next 'twang'.

The proceedings did eventually end and as I wandered through the teeming streets I was at a loss whether to feel amused, irreligious or guilty.

The ritual of the Mass goes back long before Christianity. The symbolic drinking of Christ's blood and the wafer as Christ's body is a perpetuation of the pagan cannibalistic ritual of the eating of the Chief's body and the drinking of his blood to retain his qualities. I wondered whether this was general knowledge; I doubt it!

What I did applaud was, at the end of the service, the people turned round, or crossed over to shake hands with complete strangers. I found it interesting to see this ancient pagan ritual, of the Mass followed by such a genuine, sensible lay approach to friendliness and sociability.

You may disagree with the Catholics but you can't help but like them.

XVI

From Galway the coast road to Clifden passes through Spiddall.
H.V. wrote:
'A grey land with hundreds and thousands of little stone walls. They run
up to the edge of the sky, and they fall into dips and hollows,
crisscrossing like the lines of your hand. These grey walls guard the
smallest of fields. They are not real fields, they are just bits of rock,
sprinkled with soil. Some of them are no larger than a dining table and
some of them are oblong, some square, some almost circular, some
triangular and to every one is its breast high wall.'

'Among the blue hills and the grey fields and besides the blue waters of
little loughs and on the edges of sodden peat bogs, stand small cabins,
incredibly poor and marvellously white, with hens around the door
pecking round fat black pots.'

'He hears the click of donkey's hoofs on the road and the ring of a spade
like a crowbar which men drive into the rocky soil. When the sun goes
out this place is as grey as a ghost!'

This was Connemara!
He was clearly fascinated with the place and thought of it as a country
lost in time.
When he came here in the 1930s, there were no railways, no shops, no
cars, and no telegraph poles. There were three things only: the Catholic
faith, Nature and Work. 'Connemara' he said, 'was nearer to St. Patrick
than it was to Dublin.' At the beginning of the 18th century, Ireland had a
population of about five million (more than today!) Nine out of ten lived
on farms or in small villages and made their living directly or indirectly
from agriculture. Because of this, Irishmen were very concerned about
the possession of land.

Its twenty million acres, of which only fourteen million could be farmed, was owned by about five thousand men. Some had vast estates. One man, Richard Martin, owned 200,000 acres in Connemara.

These landlords let out their land to tenant farmers who paid a rent to the landlord. If the farmer got behind with his rent, he had to do 'duty work', cutting turf or harvesting for his landlord.

Farms varied in size and the class of tenant. The most important were the 'Strong Farmers'. Between five and ten per cent of Irish tenant-farmers held thirty acres or more. These were the most prosperous men in the countryside. They held a large proportion of the best land; down the centre of Ireland.

The poorest part of the country was all down the West coast, Connemara in particular. The land was bad and the farms were usually very small.

Sooner or later, in Ireland, one will come across the word 'poteen'. It is not a word said openly and thoughtlessly. Sometimes it will slip out, followed by a sheepish and embarrassing smirk or laugh. We all know what we are talking about but there is a quiet air of mystery and subterfuge when it arises.

One night, while I was staying at a large, modern, B&B in Connemara, I asked, quite openly, in as simple and naïve a manner I could muster:
'What is this 'poteen' I've heard so much about?'
Call it brazen innocence if you like but I got away with it.

My host, a personable young man of about thirty, enlightened me and recklessly offered me a glass of that 'home-made' brew. It is Irish whiskey of course, unlicensed and very potent. Its origins, I was told, were due to licensed whiskey being too dear and also, partly to use up grain for which there was no market. The authorities, naturally disapproved of this illicit brewing and the distillers were forced to hide in the hills from the 'revenue men'.

Seventy years ago, HVMorton, struck with the same curiosity as me, tells in a more romantic way, how he found poteen.

'If you want a taste of poteen' said my friend, 'go to the place I'm telling you of and say:
'Mike O' Flaherty's black cow has died on him.'
'And is it safe?'
'It is not!'
'Will I get a taste of poteen?'
'You will …but', he added, 'for the love of Mike, if you write about it, disguise it well. You understand why…?'
'Poteen' is the most mysterious word in the country of Ireland. It is never spoken; it is always whispered.'
Time may have wiped away most of its romanticism but its eroticism still lingers on.

Connemara has changed dramatically since those pre-war days.
No longer can we hope to see bare-footed, barelegged young girls in scarlet petticoats, leaping over the stone walls, with their wicker baskets full of brown sea-weed on their backs; no longer are the myriads of white, thatched cabins sprinkled higgledy-piggledy over the countryside. All gone to be replaced by large modern bungalows.

XVII

The coastal road to Clifden is hauntingly beautiful. It has a dramatic beauty. Today, the weather is warm and sunny. The blue sky has only a few white clouds that hang over the mountain tops like tufts of white candy floss. The colours are unbelievable; the differing shades of greens, the mingling of the grey and white rocks with browns and greens and black of the land. The mountain sides rise sheer in screes; huge shadows of black move across as the sun disappears behind a cloud. The whole panorama of sea, lough, land and mountain is wonderful.
Ruins of the little white cabins can be found in the hills, scattered perhaps half a mile apart.

Today, the roads are still bumpy but they are lined with shops, restaurants, houses and bungalows: all on a grand scale, offering B&B

It is here in Connemara that one may find a speaker of the Gaelic language. Although it is now a compulsory language in schools, it seems little known. Signposts, pathetically point the way in Gaelic. No-one, including the Irish understands them.

I found a most delightful spot for B&B near a hamlet called Cashleen; a lovely little modern bungalow by the side of a Lough. Beyond, stretches the Atlantic: all around is the wild Connemara countryside. Here it was, my hostess offered to make me some genuine Irish stew. If not delicious, it was different. Again I was reminded of HV Morton's remarks about the disaster that happens between the good, wholesome food they are blessed with and its demise through the kitchen. The place is some distance from Clifden, down a narrow cart-track.

I watched the most glorious sun-set. Long after it had sunk below the horizon, its glow still lit up the hills for miles around. The effect of this combined with a full moon, made a wonderland of the whole area. Here there is a peace that defies description; it is unreal, wonderful, awe-inspiring!

On the road to Clifden is a sign pointing to 'Dan O Hara's Homestead'. The countryside is wild and rocky and here, in its midst, is an authentic, organic, old time farm, early 19th century. It is a 'theme park' with the usual audio and visual displays.

Here, in this land of tiny loughs and bogs is a memorial to commemorate the spot where the two aviators, Alcock and Brown, landed their plane after the first successful flight of the Atlantic in 1919. As I stood there on the jagged black rocks, with the turbulent waves of the great ocean surging beyond me, I pondered for a moment and tried to relive those last moments of the men as they landed. Only a few minutes before they were   hundreds of yards from land and only the deep blue sea below them. The end of their flight could have been so different!

Back on the coast road from Clifden to Claggan, down to Letterfrack and Kylemore Abbey. This impressive edifice is now a Benedictine Abbey, run by Nuns as an internationally famed boarding school for girls.

It was built by a Mr. Harry Mitchell a rich, Manchester business man. It cost one and a half million then. (today???) His wife is buried in the church, nearby. It was sold to an American millionaire, who bought it for his daughter when she married the Duke of Manchester. Sadly, they got into debt and because it was run down was sold to the nuns for £65,000.

Came to Maams Cross just to see the cottage which John Wayne used in his epic film, 'The Quiet Man'. It is strange how these works of fiction become such an attraction. It's the same with the Bronte novels, Hardy, and so on.

These cottages or cabins look so picturesque but when you think they had to be home for, often, a quite large family, something of the glamour fades and you feel pity for them. Times were hard in Connemara and life was often cruel…

Nearby is the wireless station from which Marconi transmitted the first radio message to Nova Scotia in 1907.

I move on and come to one of the few major towns in Ireland…

XVIII

Limerick. After the roads of Connemara these seem sublime. As per usual, I have left it late and it is past closing time. How different a place looks when it is empty and the shops closed and boarded up: almost as if it is sleeping and waiting for the next onslaught of humanity in the morning.

Limerick is an ancient, historical town and promises much of interest to be explored tomorrow.

Strangely enough, I think of Terry Wogan and how he developed his fat thighs by cycling over the bridge everyday! Funny?

Ever open to the tourist trade, the Irish government has undertaken a programme of restoration and many of the magnificent heritages of the past have been lovingly restored.

Here, in Limerick is a good example. King John built the castle in 1200AD and Irish Heritage has made a good job of restoring it. The exterior presents an imposing sight with its five drum towers and solid curtain walls. It is more disappointing inside but it houses a good audio-visual exhibition of the city.
A soldier's diary records the horrors of the Siege of Limerick.

It tells of one Patrick Sarsfield, the commander of the Irish forces that have been so heavily defeated by King William at the Battle of the Boyne.

King James 11 has fled to France, never to return. Sarsfield, an Anglo-Irishman decides to put Limerick in a state of siege. His army consists of 20,000 foot and 3500 mounted. The garrison works frantically to strengthen the walls, mount cannon, store ammunition.

William's army has closed all routes to the city. A deserter from the Protestant force informs Sarsfield that a siege train is on its way with huge quantities of gunpowder, cannon and pontoons.

Sarsfield, with 500 horsemen, steal out of Limerick. They reach Balyneety where the convoy has halted for the night. Having found out the password, his men draw their sabres and charge down on the sleeping convoy. The surprise attack creates havoc and the convoy is destroyed. Sarsfield returns in triumph to Limerick.

The joy is short-lived! Another siege train breaks the walls of Limerick and 10,000 storm-troopers pour into the breach. For two terrible and bloody hours the conflict raged. The citizens of Limerick: wives, daughters, tradesmen, clerks, repeatedly beat back the Royalist forces. The first siege of Limerick was beaten.

Three days later, William returned to England but the war went on.

On August the 25th the second siege began. Limerick was now the last city in Ireland held by the Jacobites. Sarsfield was still in command. He held out until October 3rd when an honourable peace was agreed.

Only a few days after the treaty was signed, a large French army arrived...too late!

Today, Limerick is a big sprawling city. Like Edinburgh, with its Georgian District and the beautiful Princes Street, Limerick, at much the same time, built a rectangular district called Newton Perry, after Mr. Sexton Perry, who became Lord Glentworth. This new town is modern Limerick; but old Limerick still exists in English Town and Irish Town. Those ancient districts face one another over a narrow piece of water. English Town had the best of it. It was built on an island and had a good castle to defend it.

The Irish Town had none of these advantages.

Visitors to Limerick must not miss seeing The Treaty Stone. It is a big rough boulder, now chipped by souvenir hunters, which stands mounted on a plinth.

The 'Honourable Peace', with which the Irish were to enjoy full civil and religious liberty and all Irish soldiers who had fought for James were to be given a free passage to France, was not kept: much to the disgrace of England.

William's victory put the Protestant ruling class in control of Ireland again. The members of this small minority, known as the Ascendancy realised that they would never be able to keep their estates and privileges without English support. Recent experiences had taught them that it was essential to leave the Catholic majority with no shred of power.

Laws were passed to prevent Catholics from ever again endangering the Protestant Ascendancy. These laws, however, were against the' spirit' of the treaty of Limerick, but the Irish parliament justified them, saying that Catholics could not be trusted while a war was being fought against France.

When peace was made, Penal Laws were defended on the ground that Catholics were loyal to the exiled Stuarts. The Irish Brigade was a constant reminder that troops were available for an invasion.

Today, Limerick is a busy, bustling place that could be likened to any other city centre, except for one thing: the shops, even the big ones, seem to be Irish and individual. The absence of such names as 'Tesco' and 'Asda', 'Lidl', and such like is noticeable and welcome!

XIX

Looking at the map, I could see Tipperary was not far away and, of course, had to be visited! Once, its name rang round the world as a song of nostalgia; even for those who had never been there. It is a reminder of the part that many Irishmen played in the First World War.

Nowhere in the Republic will you find a war memorial to those who gave their lives in the cause of freedom. England was also the enemy and these men who served it are to be forgotten; as if it never happened.

Tipperary was also the largest 'barrack' town in the U.K. When the British army withdrew, the town was left destitute and poverty stricken. It has recovered somewhat but still remains a singularly unattractive town. It has one main street. The shops are shabby and bear an air of neglect. There still lingers in the air, the old 'bad days' when Ireland was the most benighted and poverty stricken country in Europe! Today, the weather is dull and dreary, a cold, miserable drizzle has settled in. The few harassed shoppers, are scuttling about, anxious to finish their task and get home. Maybe it would all look different if it was a bright sunny day but it takes a lot of imagination to create the Tipperary that inspired the old nostalgic song. Ah well!

XX

I look at HV Morton's route. Killarney, sixty miles away, looks like the next highlight but I am sure there are treasures to be found en-route.

Sure enough, a few miles out of Limerick is Adare; a little oasis of organised, village culture. Every house is immaculate, the church is attractive and with the little thatched cottages, creates an air of well-tended loveliness. There was a local wedding going on and the people seemed much more 'upper-crust' than the usual Irish villagers. It has been described as the 'prettiest English village' in Ireland. It is not a natural 'organic' Irish village. 'Manicured' is a word that springs to mind; and indeed it is! The village owes its attractiveness to the Earl of Dunraven, who, in 1820 lovingly restored the old estate village. The village is set in a picturesque woodland setting and is well worth a detour.

The N21 to Killarney is smooth and the traffic is minimal. The countryside is pleasant, if undistinguished but that is perhaps because one is unconsciously comparing it with the dramatic scenery of Connemara and the west coast. Mile after mile goes by, passing only the odd bungalow. The little villages are set well apart and there is nothing like the straggle of houses that almost join one place to another, in England.

Killarney itself, was a bit of a shock and perhaps disappointment. Ireland seems to have been successful in conjuring up a certain romantic feeling when some of its well-known places are mentioned. It may be through a song that has become popular, world-wide or a Hollywood film dealing with the nostalgia that exiled Irishmen have become so expert in promoting.

Whatever it is, one comes to these places with a ready pre-conception of what to expect. It is not very often that the reality matches up to the dream.

August is a tourist month and, as to be expected, was busy. Stripped of its tourists, its bustling shops and restaurants, there is not much about the town to capture one's interest.

What does come as a bit of a surprise is the masses of foreign tourists of every nationality and race, of all ages and class. They jam its narrow, car-filled streets, parked bumper to bumper both sides. The teeming, endless stream tries to thread its way through the one-way centre lane. The pavements are equally throng and a moving carpet of humanity glides remorselessly along. The town has a suffocating air and one is thankful for the open shops as they operate like air-ducts to relieve the pressure that is building up. It may seem like turmoil but it is true Irish, 'Carpe Diem'. They are thinking of the long, cold, deserted streets and empty shops of winter; the shops stay open while there is trade.
"Thank God for the lakes!"

And what of the lakes themselves?

Much has been written, sung and painted about their beauty and setting but it is doubtful if anything can equal the reality of their sheer, naked beauty. Even then, you have to come to them at the right time.

HVMorton writes:
"I come through a wild gorge to the Lake of Killarney. The solitude is deathlike. There is no sound but the cry of wild birds and the bleating of black-faced sheep. There is no movement but the clouds which steam gently over the crests of the mountains. The road to Killarney winds round and up through a gorge as destitute as the Valley of the Dead in Egypt.'
I was spellbound! Behind me lay utter desolation while below me was an unearthly paradise – the Lakes of Killarney.

That was years ago but in the approach through the gorge, time is suspended and this is Ireland!

It is Sunday: nine a.m. shops are not yet open, the streets are quiet, very few cars. What a contrast to last night!

By 10 a.m. the scene has changed again. The tourists are trickling out on to the streets and some of the smaller shops were optimistically opening up.

There is increasing activity; a hiring of bikes and jaunting cars, waiting for coaches. Minute by minute, the place becomes alive again and a subdued, sleeping Killarney shakes itself for another busy day.

But it is the lakes that are Killarney and Killarney is 'the lakes'.
The lakes are the colour of the sky and as still as glass. It almost seems too good to be true: the contrast between the desolation of the gorge and the emergence into the tranquil beauty of the lakes.

The tall crests of Macgillicuddy's Reeks and the mountain of Mangerton, (an extinct volcano) of which, I was told, the crater is so deep that its water looks like black ink.

Names that can only be conjured up in Ireland; 'Devil's Punch Bowl' where the icy temperature never varies, even on the hottest summer's day.

Tales are told of the strange people that once lived in the valley: of queer, hidden places which no man really knows. And of a shy, hostile race, different from ordinary Kerry folk, who live by poaching and mix only with people of their own kind.

Tales like this you will hear all over Ireland.

When the sun is strong the hills become blue and purple and mauve. Kerry is warmer in winter than any other part of the British Isles. There are palm trees and in February, I am told, spring is already here: hedges, woodland and gorse are in full bloom and chestnut buds unfolding.

In summer, Killarney is a botanist's paradise. Where else do you get cedars of Lebanon, arbutus and wild fuchsia and other Mediterranean species in the British Isles?

Killarney has another great attraction: its boatmen! They are full of tall tales and a genius for telling you what you want to hear.

I asked the inevitable question, "Are there any leprechauns?"

"Leprechauns?" he repeated, looking hard at me.

"Why this is the most terrible place in all Ireland for them!" I was rewarded by him telling me of a farmer who had his hump-back transferred to the land-agent for some favour he had done them. The tale is told with such earnestness that to doubt it is heresy.

We say goodbye to Killarney as the sun sinks behind the mountains, the lake is silver white and mists like grey veils lie in the hollow of the hills.

Muckross House and gardens is a stately home on the borders of the middle-lake. Words are inadequate to describe this beautiful setting and on a day like this it is probably at its best.

XXI

The coast road to the Dingle Peninsula provides some spectacular views. The combination of mountain, sea, woodland and clouds present an ever-changing kaleidoscope of beauty. There is a constant change of colour as the moving clouds act as filters and shutters to the sun. The light on the sea, seems, at times, quite ethereal. There is something quite different about Ireland; one, is the multiplicity of colours that meet the eye…always changing.

In the early days of the 20th century, Ireland was looked upon, by some, as almost medieval. This was the land of the small farmer whose methods had remained unchanged for centuries. The little white cabins they called home had never seen a bath or easy way of heating water.

The Shannon Power scheme gave Ireland the most up to date electrical equipment in the world. The cows could now be milked by electricity: water could be heated at the press of a button.

It brought controversy! Instead of a universal thanksgiving, there were opposing points of view. There were those who said 'cheap electricity' would turn Ireland into another Denmark…? And that nothing will ever make Ireland an industrial nation.

German engineers were the brains and 4000 Irish labourers the muscle. They had been working on it since 1925.

The question asked was: "what is Ireland going to get out of this?"

"Foreign industry," was the reply.

"And the Irish farmer? How much is it going to cost?"

The conservatism of the Irish farmer has long roots. Electricity has come to stay but its effect, though inevitable, is much slower.

If there is one thing more than another that has moved Ireland from its centuries old sleep, it is the Common Market and European Union. Ireland has benefited and it knows it!

As we approach the Dingle it is soon evident that it was here the internationally acclaimed film, 'Ryan's Daughter', was shot. It is now a few years ago but the Dingle is still living off its fat! It is as if before, nothing existed here! From all sides and quarters one is bombarded with reminders of the 'bombshell' that hit the Dingle and altered it and its inhabitants forever!

It was a year or more in making and the trauma of the making; the real-life drama of the actors, the film crew and director, make the film itself and its powerful theme of First World War revolutionary Ireland pale beside them.

Before the Director, David Lean and the film crew arrived, the Dingle was a backwater and its inhabitants having to live a frugal sub-standard existence as small farmers and fishermen. All that vanished as munificent fees were paid for sites for shooting and undreamt of wealth for extras, crowd scenes and all the glamour of a big screen movie.

When it was all over, there was no way of returning to the old way again. The young men had learned what it was like to have money! They knew what the world outside had to offer. They left!

Here, on the gloriously wide and clear sands of Inch, tourists recall the scenes from the film: the clashes between the priest, the schoolmaster and Ryan's daughter. Everywhere you are reminded of this great event in the history of the Dingle.

Locals tell of their meeting with the stars of the film: Robert Mitchum, John Mills, Trevor Howard. A chapel contains a video, photographs and articles of clothing worn by the cast.

A replica fishing village was built on the hillside. When the film was finished, David Lean offered to leave it intact as a tourist attraction. There was no interest in the offer and it slowly fell into dereliction and decay. It was a mistake! It would have proved a great attraction but the government shied away from the expense of keeping it alive.

Kerry as the magic corner of Ireland!
It is here, in the remoteness of the mountains that go sharply down to the sea that you can understand why the belief in fairies and things not of this world still lingers.

Kerry, like the rest of Ireland has benefited from its closer links with Europe. The picture pre-war, was not a happy one. Most of the villages were small and poor. An air of despondency hung over them. The streets were empty; shop-keepers stood listlessly, waiting for customers that never appeared; there were no libraries nor village institutes; no public spirit, no money! The finger of death seemed to hang over them.

Thankfully, things have changed!

It is late afternoon and there is a break in the weather; it has started to rain; not heavy but enough to make things look damp and miserable. The magical light has gone; everything looks grey and black.

Over the hillside are some ancient dwellings, dating back to the stone-age. They are bee-hive shaped huts made from the local stone. The rain has now set in and the mountain tops are no longer visible. A curtain of rain seems to hang over the sea and everywhere around presents a damp, wet, miserable scene. It is unbelievable how a change in the weather can transform the scene.

I decided to find a place for the night on the outskirts of Tralee (or Tray-Lee, as the natives call it.)
Once again I am drawn to the place because of the age-old song and again I am disappointed. The nostalgia of Irish exiles as they romanticise about their home-land has done much for the tourist trade.

So what of Tralee, itself? It plays host to the 'Rose of Tralee' festival, in which the cultural and leisure facilities of the town are promoted. The main attraction is the theme park—the Kerry County Museum. Here one can find the 'Time-Travel' experience that takes you through Anglo-Norman times complete with the medieval smells of that time. Also, here in Tralee, is based the Siamsa Tire National Folk Theatre of Ireland. Just outside Tralee is the Biennerville Windmill, built in 1800 and still working.

The town itself was rather larger than I expected. There is a main street and one or two smaller ones leading off but the shops looked dull and uninviting. The place has an air of antiquity about it and an imposing looking church seems to have been built at their expense.

The surrounding countryside is pleasant if undistinguished. One feature that makes it different from England is the mile upon mile of bare fields, empty of any sign of life, in contrast to the cultivated fields of England with their grazing cattle and sheep.
The villages lie many miles apart and before the roads, were almost like islands, isolated from the outside world.

Found a little bungalow over-looking the bay. A curtain of rain hangs over everything. The local pubs were full of excited men, watching the semi-final of the Irish Football competition. No chance of a meal here.

At the bungalow, the lady made sandwiches and tea and introduced me to her other 'guests': a large Dutch couple and a German. They all spoke perfect English: a fact which never ceases to amaze me.

The evening passed pleasantly, the conversation wide and topical. They were very amused at my attempts to entertain them with a broad Yorkshire accent.

The morning broke bright and sunny but by 9.30 the rain-clouds were here again, with the sun only allowed to break through intermittently. It is cold, wet and windy.

Close by Tralee is the little hamlet of Blennerville, once a port of some importance before the canal to Tralee reduced it to nothing. It was from here during the great famine that thousands fled their homeland, never to return. The sad story is re-lived in an audio-visual presentation at The Blennerville Windmill Visitor & Craft Centre.

Tourists who come to see the old white-washed thatched cottages of the Hollywood films will be disappointed. They can only be found in the Theme Parks now. In their place are modern bungalows: all set well back from the road and occupying anything from half an acre to five acres. They are, without exception, immaculate! Inside they are well furnished and up to date with every modern convenience.

Some of the little villages around Tralee are worth visiting. Ballyduff is one of them. It is here the Rattoo Heritage is established. This is a body pledged to protect, promote and preserve the historic, cultural and environmental aspects of the kingdom of Kerry.

XXII

The road to Macroom is an enchantment. It runs along the mountain side and gives a wonderful vista of the lakes. We come to Kenmare. It is August, the busiest month of the year for tourism. A busy, bustling little town. The shops are small and varied but all throng with tourists. The pavements are crowded as the endless throng moves along, like a snaking carpet of humanity: so different from the depressed place that Morton visited pre-war.

The road winds its way down to beautiful Glengariff at the head of Bantry Bay. Here, if one wants peace and tranquillity is the perfect spot. There still lingers an unequalled air of Victorian gentility. The Queen herself is reputed to have stayed at the Eccles Hotel and George Bernard Shaw supposedly wrote, his 'St. Joan' here.

Part of the magic of Glengariff, is Garinish Island. G.B.S. was enchanted by it. Locals maintain that it was here that he found inspiration for much of his work. We do not expect to see an exotic Italian garden with pergolas, rock gardens and a marble pond full of goldfish. The place is landscaped with neo-classical follies and planted with subtropical flora. Exotic shrubberies, beautiful beds of camellias, azaleas and rhododendrons abound.
All this man-made beauty contrasts with natural beauty of the wild sea-scape and barren mountains beyond.

The island was turned into this exotic garden by a business man called Harold Peto in 1910.

I remember reading one of Spike Milligan's books on Irish poems and running across the Micro-chephalic community of Macroom. While one always had to take Spike with a dose of salt, I could not avoid slaking my curiosity when it lay in my path. I was disappointed! Much of these southern Irish villages are the same and although not carrying that dead air of depression that Morton saw in the thirties, have not altered that much. The inhabitants seemed neither worse nor better than any others. Oliver Cromwell granted the castle to William Penn, whose son went on to found the American state of Pennsylvania.

XXIII

Cork, the Republic's second largest city, is not like any other town in Ireland. Indeed, it is simply not like any other town; it is unique! What makes it so?

Ireland's second largest city stands on an island in the River Lee.

Most of the major buildings date from the late 1800's. The lack of any older buildings may be attributed to the fact that the city always seemed to back the losing side in the historical conflicts it lived through. They supported Perkin Warbeck in his rebellion against Henry V11; they supported Charles against Cromwell and in 1690 threw in their lot with the hapless James 11. After this last disaster, much of the city's medieval and Tudor buildings were demolished. It was in 1920, at the height of 'the troubles' that half of Cork was burnt down.

Today, Cork is recognised as the undisputed cultural capital of southern Ireland. HVMorton described it as the most foreign city he had seen in Ireland, not in appearance but in atmosphere.
The people of Cork are different from people in other parts of the country. They are clannish and for centuries have intermarried within its boundaries. It has its own distinctive 'Cork' accent.

The women of Morton's visit, with their traditional black head-shawls have vanished and replaced by the bright young things found in every big city in the world.

XXIV

The Blarney Stone.
It is a fact that wherever you may be in the world, if you mention the word, 'Blarney', you have made 'some' communication.

They may or may not have heard of the 'Blarney Stone' but in one context or another, 'Blarney' opens a door.

How, we must ask, does this come about? It is not on account of everyone knowing or having visited this obscure and unpretentious little village near Cork, or has performed that uncomfortable and semi-dangerous business of kissing the Blarney Stone.

Perhaps we shall never know the true origins but the one that is most popular is the tale of one, Lord Blarney, a young, handsome frequenter of Elizabeth's Court, who while managing to keep the Queen on a friendly, flirtatious acquaintance, had never got round to swearing his oath of allegiance to her. He always had a flow of Irish banter to put her off. At times she would lose her temper and cry:
"Oh no! I can't listen to that Blarney, any more!"

It stuck! and now anyone that wishes to have that 'gift of the gab' or easy flow of Irish banter, has only to kiss the Blarney Stone to get it.

It is unfortunate that the stone is situated at the top of the castle's turret and to kiss it one has first, to toil up the exhausting trek of the steep, spiral stone staircase to reach it. The stone itself is quite inaccessible to reach alone. While someone holds your legs, you have to lie on your back and lean backwards over a 150 foot drop to, 'upside down', give the stone a kiss.

This precious 'gift of the gab' is something I am sure all the Irish possess already.

In the evening I drove back to Cork again to try and re- capture the flavour of the place. It was not a successful venture. The shops were closed and although there were plenty of cars, non-stop flowing through the streets, an empty city is not an inspiring sight: decidedly unattractive, to say the least.

There are still the rows and rows of dirty, old terrace houses and the whole area looked rundown and neglected.

I returned to Blarney and was persuaded to visit the village hall where there was to be an evening of Irish music and dance. It was well attended and soon the place was alive with a gusto of merriment, song and laughter unequalled by any but the Irish.

Bought a raffle ticket and won a bottle of Irish Whiskey. At every announcement of a lucky winner, one had to say from what part of the world you came and a hearty round of applause followed. When after hearing a lot of Irish and American place-names, I sheepishly uttered, 'Sheffield, Yorkshire, England.'

I remember thinking the clapping was decidedly muted. Perhaps I was wrong...I hope so.

I found a pleasant little B&B where I met two Americans, on the same mission as myself. They were from Nebraska and were interested to learn I had followed the sesquicentennial of the Oregon Trail. We should have started from St.Louis but due to unprecedented flooding we had to by-pass that and start from Ogallalla.

It makes me sad when I think of the long history of struggle and conflict between the two countries so geographically and historically tied together. Today, Ireland has only half its population of a hundred years ago. I would safely say that there are more Irish people in the U.K. than there are in Ireland. If you think of the U.S.A. particularly Boston and New England, the influence they carry throughout the world is quite disproportionate to their numbers.

It comes as no surprise to learn that the number of American tourists outnumbers all the rest. They are coming home!

Blarney, on a fine, warm, sunny August morning is a delightful place to be in. The large open Village Green has a row of old-fashioned white-washed cottages on one side and bordering the other side are some large, well-kept houses and hotels.

On its main street are a collection of non-descript little shops dominated by a modern super-market. The whole village is surrounded by the heavily wooded Park entrance to the Castle grounds. Altogether, an enchanting little spot.

The Blarney Woollen Mill is a huge building that looks as if it might have been the home of a wealthy person at one time. The interior is a veritable treasure trove of expensive crystal and woollen goods of every description plus the usual little souvenirs.

It was midday before we left Blarney; it has not changed much over the years and long may it remain so.

The last time I was here, nearly twenty years ago, Ireland had an unemployment figure of 10%. I suspect, since its entry into the Common Market and now the European Community, things are much better.

XXV

Like in the U.K. the Public Houses, even in a depression, are always well supported. Restaurants too, do not show any signs of a depression.

Ireland has now a flourishing tourist trade and during the summer months of July and August it becomes a cauldron of languages in search of its many treasures. Predominant among them is Italian; it is the Ecclesiastical style of architecture that is the lure.

My next venue - Mount Melleray. It took me via country lanes through villages too tiny to put on a map. I knew one could stay here for the night and the idea of sleeping in a monastery cell was appealing, so it was with a breath of excitement I made my way there. It was not that easy! What few sign-posts there were did not seem all that reliable. I came across an old man, who by his appearance, somewhat resembled Michael, the village idiot in 'Ryan's Daughter'. I did not have much confidence in his directions but he spoke quite sensibly and directed me. When he left me to enter his big five bedroomed bungalow set in its two acres of ground, with flower- beds, lawn and a long white gravel drive, I wondered again, how have these ostentatiously poor farmers with their tiny dairy farms managed to build such fine houses, often on, or near the site of their mean little cabins. The answer, I was told, was the 'Common-Market' plus money from America.

Further down the winding, twisting lanes, nearly always so over-lapped with trees that it is like driving through a tunnel, the dairy herds became more numerous now but I still noticed the absence of any arable farming.

Just before Mount Melleray is a holy grotto. I am not sure what, if any, miracle occurred here but there were lots of cars and several elderly people seemed to be paying homage to someone or something.

Mount Melleray is an impressive Cistercian monastery. They were an old order that was driven out of France. Here, a hundred men have taken a vow of Life-long silence and are living high up in the, mountains of County Waterford in this Trappist monastery. They are men of many nationalities and experience.

It was late evening when I climbed the steep hill to Mount Melleray. The monks were returning from their rich farm-lands. I stopped one and asked him the way to the Guest-house. He placed a finger to his lips and shook his head but he pointed with his hand and following his directions, I turned a corner and came to the guest-house.
I rang the bell and a middle-aged lay-brother came.
"Good evening," he said, "can I help you?"
I was taken aback for a moment and replied:
"I'm sorry, are you allowed to speak?"
"I am absolved from my vow while in charge of my guests."
"Can I stay for the night then?"
"You can stay the night, or a week or a month, if you like."
You could see that time meant nothing to him at all.

The Trappists at Mount Melleray hold open house to the world. Any man or woman -of any faith -may stay there as long as they like. No one is ever asked to pay anything but it is expected one leaves a donation in a box, if they can afford to do so; if not, they are sent away with a blessing.

Mount Melleray is the only monastery in Ireland which will offer shelter to a woman.

I would like to stay the night but I must be in Cork tomorrow morning.
"Cork!" he cried, "why that must be forty miles away."
"Yes," I replied,"but I have an appointment with some drisheen."
"Drisheen?" he echoed. "I don't hear that word very often."

I followed him into the bare hall of the guest house. Was I imagining it? No, there was a distinctive 'religious' smell, compounded of bare walls, old rugs, stale incense and furniture polish.
"Now," said the lay brother, "will you read the list of rules and then sign your name in the visitors' book."
I cast a quick eye over the printed list and signed the book.

"Now," said the monk, "I will show you to your cell."
We mounted the flight of wooden stairs from the hall. On the first
landing he opened a door and carried my suit-case into a room. The
room surprised me. I had hoped for and expected a real, genuine,
monk's cell. It was a cell only in name!
There was a bed that proved to be more comfortable than any hotel I had
slept in, in Ireland. It was furnished in greater luxury that could be
found in any County Town hotel. There was a ward-robe, a wash-stand
and a table, all made by the monks. The walls were bare, save for a large
crucifix, beneath which was a 'faldstool'.

Again, in silence, the monk helped me unpack my little bundle of
vanities: razor, shaving soap, powder and my pyjamas.

When we had finished, he left me saying,
"You will now examine your conscience for an hour."

I quote from H.V. Morton -
My 'cell' was immediately above the porch of the Guest-House. There
was a small window of gothic design and the panes were very small.
There was a narrow window-seat on which I sat, looking down into a
beautiful Italianate garden. It was a walled garden enclosed by tall trees.
There were several cypress trees, and against the gloom of their foliage
were life-size statues of the Virgin Mary, standing out, startlingly white.

It was a hot summer's evening. The birds were singing and the bees
were busy in the flowers. I felt restless and wondered what people in
London were doing at this moment. People hurriedly scrambling their
way home after a dreary and tiring day in the city, or dressing for
dinner, parties assembling in hotels, waiters with wine-lists, half-clad
women sweeping into restaurants and theatres, actors and actresses
putting on their make-up for the evening's performances and all
embraced in the mad dance of life. I envied them not!

I noticed a figure in the garden. A Trappist in a white habit and a black
scapular was walking slowly round, his hands held before him but
hidden in long sleeves, his head bent to the ground. His walk was
monotonous and habitual. He was as unconscious he was walking as he

was unconscious that he was in the garden. I could see his lips were moving. There was something terrible in his concentration. I wondered who, and what, he was before he entered this spiritual prison. Somewhere in the world was there a woman who was once his wife or lover. He looked a man in the prime of life. What if they could see him now, living only for death.

Another figure entered the garden; it was an aged monk. He walked round in the same attitude of whispered prayer. They passed each other but neither heeded the other. I watched them fascinated. They had through meditation lifted themselves to another plane.

I sat by my little window, thinking how strange it was that in passing through a gate I should have found myself in the Middle-ages. All my Catholic ancestors rose up in me to recognise the 'Peace of the Church'; all my Protestant ancestors rose up and fought them tooth and nail, so that between them I sat looking into the garden in a strangely muddled sort of mind, knowing only that I appreciated from the bottom of my heart the sincerity and the immortal hunger of these men.

The hour's meditation seemed endless. To think, these monks spent their lives in silent meditation. It was the silence of the place that worked on my nerves: a silence that had soaked itself into the very stones; a silence which even the trees seemed conscious; a silence that was the forerunner of death!

There was a book on the table; 'The Confessions of St. Augustine. I turned over the leaves and found scribblings by previous occupants. Some were sentences in almost hasty, drunken script, that trailed off the page.

"Blessed Mary, pray for me!" I read on one; and on another, written in marking-ink pencil, lividly blue in patches, as though they were the writer's tears,
"I am a miserable sinner---pray for me!"
I closed the book with the unpleasant feeling I had put my ear to a key-hole.

It was all so silent, the trees standing in a windless evening, a robin singing his lovely elegy to a dying day, sharp and crystal clear. Each note high and rounded. The sun was sinking but it would be hours before the dusk fell. I heard the lowing of cattle; the monks driving their herds from the pasture to their byre.

The door opened. The lay Brother stood there. The hour was over.
"Follow me," he said.
He led me downstairs. We left the guest house and came into a stone corridor. I could smell incense and knew that we were going back to the chapel for compline. We stood back to allow the brotherhood to pass us.

The monks live on the most frugal diet and drink only water. Over the years, Mount Melleray has become famous for curing dipsomania and many alcoholics have come here for a cure.

I followed the monk on his tour of the monastery.
"This is the buttery, we give food and drink to anyone that asks for it."

We were in a long stone passage. A bell overhead began to toll.
There was a queer shuffling of feet on the stone, then, round the corner came a procession of cowled figures walking with bent heads, two by two, first the priests in coarse white gowns, then the lay brothers, in brown habits girdled at the waist with a chord. Not one looked up as they passed. They went into the chapel for their evening prayers and the doors closed silently behind them.

As they passed me I tried to catch a glimpse of their faces to see if it gave me any clue of who and what they were before they disappeared from their fellow-men beneath their cowls.

What had they known of life? No one can say. Once they had names by which the world knew them, now they are Brother Dominic, Brother Paul, Brother Aloysius.

They have voluntarily cut themselves off from life and now merely live in an ante-chamber to death.

The silence of Mount Melleray is almost frightening! Cowled figures brush past one in dim corridors like ghosts.

I wondered. Do they never wish to speak? Do they never wish to exchange a thought with a fellow-man?

The refectory was a bare chilly room, with a pulpit in the centre beside one wall. Long wooden tables were set round the room and at each table a wooden bench. Beside each place were two tin mugs and a plate. Leaning against each plate was a card with the monk's name written on it in large letters.

In the library upstairs the monk told me the history of the monastery. In 1830 a band of Trappist monks expelled from France arrived on the barren slopes of the Knockmealdown mountains with one shilling and ten pence between them! They made some kind of a shelter and a little oratory. The peasants came from the hills to do a day's work for them. Their farm-lands grew. They became known for their good works. Rich men made wills for them in their favour, and so, gradually and within one hundred years, the penniless settlement has grown into a large, prosperous and wealthy community.

They have done in Ireland what their predecessors did in England in the barren Yorkshire moors and dales, at Fountains, Rievaulx and Jervaulx.

They have made what was once a wilderness, a place of corn and fruit and grass where fat cattle graze.

We went into the garden and into the grounds. There are rows of open graves: it is part of a Trappist's duty to dig his own grave.

As we parted, the lay-brother said,
"Good-bye. Pray for me tonight and I will pray for you."

A simple thing but if everyone did it, how different the world might be.

Visiting the monastery had stirred me and I found sleep difficult.

The friend with whom I was to dine told me of their innumerable good deeds.

He called himself a 'bad Catholic'. He had nothing but scorn for the parish priests. 'The blackbirds' as he called them, had done nothing but keep the country in a condition of superstition and illiteracy.

I recalled the comment I heard in Clifden;
"Thank God, we are getting rid of the priests!"

Many years ago, a novelist called Robert Hichens wrote a book called, 'The Garden of Allah.' I believe I saw the film, with Marlene Dietrich as the star.

The novel tells of a Trappist monk who flees from the monastery and encounters the problems of life in the world outside. He recalls the horror of the monastery, with its silent monks, its denial of all the things we call happiness but my slight glimpse into Mount Melleray told me that the ancient 'Peace of the Church' lay over it. It is a sanctuary. It is everything that was good and sincere in the Middle Ages. It is true, the uncompromising severity of it frightened me a little but it also attracted me. I feel an urge to go back again and find out for myself what life is really like behind those silent walls.

There were two incidents that linger in my mind, that reminded me that with all its precious air of Holiness and 'out of this world' atmosphere, it still has its feet firmly planted in the real world too.

As you leave the Monastery you have to pass through 'The Shop'. Here laid out as professionally as any Marks & Spencers was a complete Treasure Trove of Holy articles. Not only that but also mementoes of the history of nearby Cobh: its role in the great emigration, the sinking of the Lusitania at nearby Kinsale and the Titanic, where this was its last port of call before its ill fated maiden voyage.

The other thing was the 'Confession' cubicle. When Catholic friends have mentioned about going to confession, I always thought how very shrewd and down to earth are these priests.

They realise how essential it is that human nature has to unburden its mind, sometimes over the most trivial of things that they cannot communicate to their closest friend.

The confession box is where they can really let themselves go, secure in the knowledge their secrets are safe and whatever the confession, it is received with understanding and assurance that   they will be forgiven. Even confessing to a heinous crime like murder can never be revealed.

An old man, not too sober, it appeared, was having to struggle with a couple of monks to fight his way to confession. Such is the hold of the Catholic faith.

Wexford. Here crossed Strongbow to conquer Ireland

Typical Irish scattered village

Irish cabin

A weaver's cottage

A typical modern B&B

Knock

Cashel of the Kings

Cahir Castle

Cahir Castle, at the door

Cahir House Hotel (Butler family home)

Town centre, Cahir

The Author and fresh Irish mussels

Kenmare

Blarney Castle

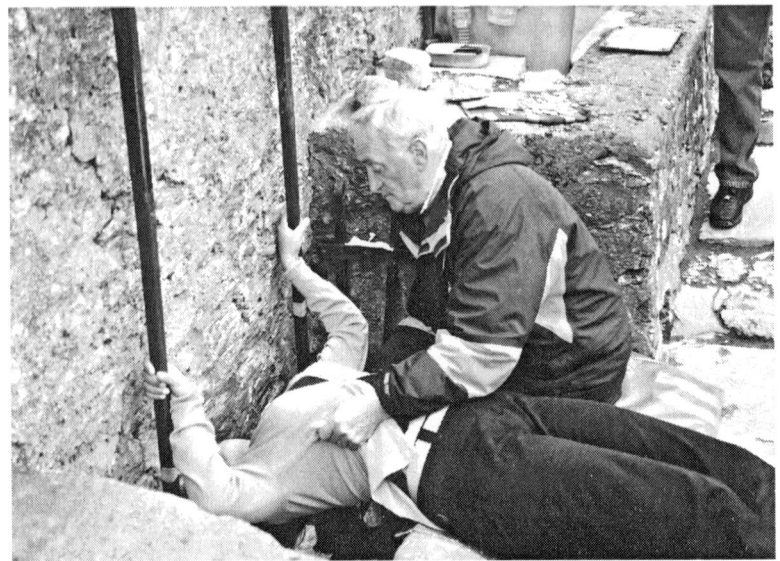

Kissing the Blarney Stone

Dingle - the sands at Inch

"cosmetic" Adare

Cong

The Jack Doyle pub

Cobh harbour

A Glimpse of Old Ireland

Cinderella in Connemara (W.J.Henley,Wembley)

The Claddagh, Galway (Independent Newspapers Ltd)

Fair Day (Thomas Mason, Dublin)

XXVI

My destination was now Cobh, (pronounced Cove). Many years ago, in London, I had met a jolly young man called James Connolly. He used to say, with some pride, that he was a kinsman of THE James. However, what impressed me more was his claim to know Jack Doyle, a well-known heavy-weight boxer, who also came from Cobh.

I moved on, down winding country lanes, through little villages hard to find on a map. I had an image in my mind about Cobh. It is described as an island in Cork harbour. Therefore, while still driving and aware of the vast Atlantic alongside of me, I was surprised to find I had entered Cobh. It was obviously the scale of the harbour that had misled me. It is huge. Here it was, the great liners anchored: waiting for the hordes of impoverished emigrants, desperate to escape from their blighted homeland to seek a new life on the other side of the world.

Cobh has been described as the saddest spot in Ireland.

I am sure, today, folk in N. Ireland, after forty years of violence can claim precedence over that. Nevertheless, one has only to remember that it was from here that a million or more young Irish men and women boarded the great liners waiting for them in deep Atlantic waters to start a new life in America and parts of the Commonwealth.

Cobh has been called,
"a wound that Ireland cannot staunch; a haemorrhage of her best and youngest blood".

In their book, 'Ireland', over a century ago, Mr. and Mrs. C.S. Hall, give a vivid description of the scene of embarkation. It is heart-rending.
'We stood in the month of June on the quay at Cork to see some emigrants embark in one of the steamers for Falmouth, on the way to Australia. The crowd of exiles amounted to two hundred and an immense crowd had gathered to bid them a long and last adieu. The scene was touching to a degree; it was impossible to witness it without a

heart-pain and tears. Mothers hung upon the necks of their athletic sons, young girls clung to elder sisters. Fathers, old, white-headed men fell on their knees with arms uplifted to heaven, imploring the protection of the Almighty on their departing children.

"Och," exclaimed one aged woman. "All's gone from me in the wide world when you're gone! Sure, you were all I had left! Of seven sons - but you! O Dennis, Dennis, never forget your mother - don't adorneen - your poor ould mother - your poor old mother, Dennis."

And Dennis, a young man, though the sun was shining on his grey hair, supported his mother in his arms until she fainted, and then he lifted her into a small car that had conveyed his baggage to the vessel, and kissing a weeping young woman who leaned against the horse, he said: "I'll send home for you both, Peggy, in the rise of next year."

If Cobh did not meet with my expectations, being very much like any little sea-side town, I was here and it must be explored.
I stopped outside a B&B notice in the main street. It didn't look very salubrious but it was there and I wanted to get out and see the town.

Rising up from its promenade is the steepest street I have ever encountered. It is steeper than the one at Haworth, in Yorkshire, which claims to be the steepest. It is a tasking climb.

The huge neo-Gothic St. Colman's Cathedral stands here -overlooking the town but I did not stop; I was eager to find the 'Jack Doyle' public house. It was way over the top. When I got there it was a blaze of light and noise.

Inside was crammed with Irishmen, doing very much the same as English men, or all men, the world over: enjoying their beer and the companionship of an all male gathering. There was not a woman present and I got the impression that the women-folk of Cobh were not welcome.

There were lots of photographs of Jack round the walls but it seemed time had dimmed his memory and eventually he would be forgotten except for those like myself, fascinated by the sport.

I returned to Cork for an important luncheon engagement. I had mentioned the word 'Drisheen' and if the word 'poteen' evoked caution and mystery, 'Drisheen' brought forth laughter. I was puzzled.

Drisheen is a dish peculiar to Cork. I was anxious to try it. When it was brought to me I thought it looked like a large and poisonous snake I had seen in a zoo. This one originates from Cork. It is said that whenever a Corkonion travels away on business, he always takes a yard of drisheen with him.

Drisheen is a kind of sausage made from sheep's blood and milk. You might say it is the Irish cousin to Lancashire Black Pudding.

They say in Cork that when you are ill, doctors recommend it because it is the most nourishing and digestible of all foods. It looks a bit like a firm chocolate blancmange.

XXVII

On my way to Mount Melleray, I had spotted a sign-post pointing to Fermoy. My interest was immediately aroused. In my capacity as a Sports Teacher I had taken a group of youngsters to compete in a National Sports meeting in Norfolk. Notable, among the dignitaries and local aristocracy attending was Lord Fermoy, with his wife and daughter. They sat down on the front bench alongside me and my group. I didn't realise then, that this young girl would one day be the mother of Princess Diana. As for Fermoy...I had no idea where it was. I resolved to pay it a visit later. It proved to be a pleasant little town, very popular for its fishing. It had no great history: being founded by a rich Scottish Merchant, John Anderson, in 1789. It was, at one time, a garrison town for the British Army.

The original Lord Fermoy lost the estate, along with his fortune in a single night's gambling.

This countryside is enchanting. Miles and miles of little country lanes with only, now and again, a tiny picturesque village. There are no sprawling housing estates, no dull suburbs that spread their ugly tentacles from one town to another, making it impossible to distinguish their boundaries. Nothing but miles of green fields and hedges. The farms are quite large dairy farms with their herds of cows grazing on the luscious grass. How different, I think, from the skimpy farms in the West, where a few cows may be seen grazing in the small fields surrounding the bungalows.

Here, on the banks of the broad, slow Blackwater - a mighty salmon stream, rises the truly magnificent Castle of Lismore. It reminds me of the other magnificent Warwick Castle, in England. The huge courtyard is awe-inspiring, while the view from the drawing-room is terrifying in its aspect.

History tells us that it was here that the defeated James II spent the night after his flight from the Battle of the Boyne.

Lismore town itself has that distinctive air of a 19th Century estate town. It is now a designated Heritage Town but still the Irish home of the Dukes of Devonshire since 1753. Previous to that it was in the hands of Sir Walter Raleigh who then sold it to Richard Boyle, later Earl of Cork, whose fourteenth child was Robert, the celebrated chemist and formulator of Boyle's Law. He was actually born in the castle.

Parts of the castle date back to King John but in the early 19th Century the 6th Duke of Devonshire extensively re-modelled it.

It intrigues me how, bearing in mind the conflicts between the two countries that Ireland still allows the old English land-lords to flourish. Although the house is not open to the public, the Lismore Heritage Centre recounts the history of the town since its foundation AD 636.

I was eager to see Clonmel, for several reasons. Firstly, it was here that the writer, Lawrence Sterne, was born. His classic, 'Tristram Shandy' is often claimed to be the first English novel.
His father was stationed here as an officer in the Army. His son, Lawrence, wrote the novel while incumbent at Coxwold, a village in North Yorkshire. It is a humorous account of the life of a country parson in the 18th century. 'Shandy Hall', where he lived is now a 'must' for literary enthusiasts.
It was here in Clonmel where Anthony Trollope worked as Post Master General for the GPO. George Borrow, another famous novelist, went to school here. However, it was also on a more personal level, I wished to visit the place. Some years ago, while working in a large Comprehensive/Community School, I met a young Irishman who was on the staff. He was leaving to take up a post at a school in Clonmel.

He told me why he had decided to move back to Ireland. He was married with two children. His wife was also teaching but they found with both of them working, the time with their young family was limited.

In Ireland he would receive a married man's allowance plus allowances for the children. Financially they would be nearly as well off and his wife could stay at home to look after the young ones.

He had found a pleasant house in Clonmel only a short distance from the school. He could walk to work. Clonmel sounded a lovely place to live, certainly more attractive than the mining town in South Yorkshire where he was now.

I listened fascinated while he eulogised on his new appointment. I asked him to let me know if a vacancy should come up. He shook his head, looking rather sadly I thought.

"I don't think it would be easy," he said.

"Why?" I queried.

"You're not a Catholic, are you?"

"No," I replied. "What difference does that make?"

He pursed his lips, then said, "Catholic schools. It would be unlikely you'd stand a chance."

"But you are a Catholic in a Protestant school here. What's the difference?"

He shrugged his shoulders.

"Perhaps I'm wrong; I hope so but religion plays a big part in Ireland."

If Kildare can boast to be a Horse Centre, with its National Stud at Tully Farm and the nearby famous Curragh Racecourse, Clonmel can claim to be the centre for the Greyhound World. These famous pedigree racing dogs can be seen exercising, like the horses at Kildare.

Clonmel proved to be a really delightful little town and one I could gladly live in.

XXVIII

Cahir lies a few miles west of Clonmel and I couldn't wait to get there! When I first read HV Morton's account of his visit there in the 1930s, I was captivated by it. He wrote -

I like the town of Cahir. I like to stand at an upstairs window of the excellent, homely hotel which was once a private house and watch the slow life of the wide main street.

'There is nothing in it but a few old people mysteriously congregated with their donkey carts, standing engaged in conversation and earnestly discussing the price of vegetables. It is a curious watchful street. Although it is often empty it is never asleep. It is as wide as a parade ground, and I imagine that anything happening on it is immediately known all over the town.

Irish country towns vary enormously in atmosphere. Some seem drenched in a hopeless shabbiness. It would be impossible to do any work in them. The only thing would be to drink and gloom and make excuses to yourself. But a few miles from such towns are others surprisingly different – bright, clean, hopeful, vaguely busy. Cahir is like this.

Down the main street comes a herd of cows Fine horses go by with plaited manes and tails and numbered cards on their flanks. There is a cattle and horse show somewhere near. A sable priest stands at the corner of the street, and pauses in his conversation to follow the horse-flesh with his eyes; as in fact, everyone does. It is all so peaceful and so drenched in the sanity of the eighteenth century.

The warm afternoon sunlight falls over the square. Down the road comes a man leading a great black bull. There is a ring through its nostrils. Its hide shines like polished ebony. It sways under the weight of its fat and muscle, placing its feet on the road as deliberately as an elephant, and as it goes by it turns its head now and then and looks with unconscious fierceness around it.

A bell tolls. It is the Angelus.

The man and bull come to a standstill. The herdsman lifts his shabby hat and bends his head in prayer. The great beast stands rock-still beside him. An old man leading a donkey in a cart, lifts his cap. Two men who might be commercial travellers or solicitors cross themselves and the whole town prays.'

A picture in words, as vivid as any portrait or photograph!

HVM goes on to comment on the Angelus.

'The moment of the Angelus is, to me, the most touching and the most beautiful in an Irish day. At first a stranger is unaware of the bell. He may be riding in a Dublin tram-car. Suddenly there is a movement. Men and women are making the sign of the cross. Or in crowded street the man you are talking to becomes silent and lifts his hat. But it is in the lanes and the country towns of Ireland that the Angelus is most beautiful.

This silent communion with God at morning, noon and sunset, coming as it does in the midst of life and the business of life, summoning men at work in fields, in cities and in towns to pause in whatever they may be doing and turn their thoughts to the throne of God, is an expression of the underlying spirituality of Irish life.'

The 'homely hotel' referred to turned out to be the one time family home of the Butlers who, built the castle as a stronghold but as the turbulent times receded, built themselves the substantial 'Town House' where HV Morton stayed and described the view from his room.

Now, I stand here, in that same room, gazing with some awe at that same town square before me ...but how so different!

'Slow life!'...Instead of the donkey carts and a few rustics engaged in discussing the price of vegetables, the square is now a maelstrom of endless streams of traffic polluting the warm country air with its toxic fumes and smothering the adventurous shoppers in a blanket of noise and turmoil.

This is Cahir, mid-day, August 2009

There are no cows, no horses, no fine black bulls; only the same, untidily dressed horde of shabby jeans and sweat-shirts to be seen anywhere in the world. Is this what they mean by 'Globalisation'?

While I feel a sense of disappointment, in one way, I also acknowledge the way it has dragged itself out of the 19th century ...thanks to the European Union.

Considering Cahir is such a small town it is admirably served with facilities for an evening meal. I chose an Italian one with an Italian chef. A group of young Italian girls came in, all of a giggle. They spoke excitedly to the chef, in Italian of course.

The pizza was excellent and I left in search of some Irish music. Found 'The Tavern' where a notice informed me, 'Traditional Irish Music' was due to start at 9.30p.m .

Quite a crowd had gathered and an interesting collection it appeared. Seated round the bar, on high stools, sat about a dozen older men: grey-haired, sober-suited, average about sixty-five perhaps. They sat there talking quietly or silent with serious expressions on their faces.
At one time I would have thought that their conversation would have been the eternal struggle to throw off the English yoke. But no! From little scraps of information I picked up, it was all about last night's semi-final between Mayo and Donegal and the latest English soccer results!

Scattered around the lounge-bar were groups of youngsters between eighteen and twenty. They were mostly girls, in clusters of two or three. I noticed one tall, good-looking young woman surrounded by a small group of admiring friends. Some of these Irish girls can be very attractive.

There are some that are the archetypal, long black hair type with the blue eyes you can find nowhere else but in Ireland. Then, there are the other, equally Irish type with long, ginger wavy hair and green eyes.

Alas, there are also plenty of the other, universally bland type, like anywhere in Northern Europe.

I could not help but ponder why so many young attractive girls were here alone.

About 10.30.p.m. with the Irish band still absent and to my amazement no comment made on the fact, I rather timidly asked if they might ever appear.

"Sure, it's a possibility sir. They aren't to an hour or so."

Later that evening, a group of young men trooped in and made straight for their respective girl-friends who had been patiently waiting two or three hours for them. The young men were an untidy looking bunch: rather shoddy and down at heel. If they appeared rather smaller and less robust than their English counterparts, they were also more placid and less noisy.

When I decided, 'enough was enough', I left, with still no appearance of the 'Irish Music'.

Cahir Castle.
I was eager to see the castle, the strong- hold, of the Butlers for centuries.
I was not disappointed; it is an impressive sight.
It is sited on a small island on the River Suir.

The Irish government, in line with its policy of restoration, has done Cahir proudly. I remember HV Morton's comments when he was here.
He said:
'If I owned this castle and had the money to indulge a fantasy I would restore it and furnish the finer rooms in it with armour and furniture of the period.'

I hope he lived to see those dreams become a reality.

The young girl guide was both erudite and entertaining; you felt she had an affinity with the place. When I told her I was an Irish Butler and had been to one of the 'Butler clan' gatherings in Kilkenny (they came from all over the world, including some Arabs) she jokingly remarked; 'Oh. Have you come to re-claim your title?'

I shall not forget Cahir... I like it.

XXIX

On my way to Cashel I visited the 'Folk Village' a collection of little, thatched, white-washed 'cabins' and artefacts of the past.

Among the exhibits was an old Gypsy caravan, eighty five years old and in use until 1986. It was the home of a family of tinkers: parents and fourteen children. The small children slept in the caravan with their parents, in a cupboard under their bed, while the older children slept outside.

The inside looked deceptively roomy. A notice on the wall informed how the tinkers came to be 'travelling folk'. It read: 'The Tinkers were the richest people in the land and that is why their lands were seized and they were forced to become 'travellers'. Considering the utter poverty of the Irish peasant, I can well believe the tinkers were better off, if only by comparison.

In conversation with my land-lady of that night, she admitted that it was only after the entry into the Common-Market and E.E.C. that Ireland began to pull itself out from the centuries of poverty and misery.

Again, I was told how the Government, with huge grants from the E.E.C. had subsidised these fine bungalows and houses on condition they became quasi B&B for tourists. Tourism must now be among Ireland's largest industries.

Here was a typical old fashioned 'cabin', with white-washed mud and wattle walls and thatched roof. Inside was surprisingly spacious. A large, open fire-place with peat burning merrily away warmed the room and delighted the nostrils with its aroma.

An immense black iron kettle swung permanently over the blaze. A large, crude, 'goose-dresser' with its rows of cups and 'jam-jugs', (jam was so expensive they had to take a jug to buy a measure.) The 'goose-dresser' was so called because of the large space underneath, reserved for the goose to lay her eggs.

There were replicas or originals of an old-style butcher's shop a blacksmith's forge and a room containing pictures, newspaper cuttings, and relics and artefacts from the 1916 rebellion. It was all very captivating if a little amateurish.

The old lady care-taker seemed willing to talk and inevitably the talk veered on to the 'troubles' in the North. She was vehement in her condemnation of the I.R.A. so much so that I began to think; 'the Lady doth protest too much.'

She was of the firm conviction that Capital Punishment, shooting or hanging should be re-instated. Thinking of the mis-guided shooting of the 1916 Uprising and its consequence of turning the rebels into martyrs, I refrained from comment.

When I learned, later, there was a strong I.R.A. 'cell' in Cashel I was not surprised.

XXX

Cashel of the Kings, as it is known, is a natural rocky formation that rises dramatically out of the plain of Tipperary. It was a symbol of royal and priestly power for over a thousand years.

It was the seat of the Kings of Munster from the 5th Century.
In 1101, they handed over Cashel to the church and it flourished as a religious centre until a siege by Cromwell's army in 1647 culminated in the massacre of its 3000 occupants.

The place was finally abandoned in the late 18th Century. Now, two hundred or more years on, it is besieged again: this time by tourists from all over the world.

Although the castle has lost some of its splendour, Cormac's Chapel is still standing and is one of the most outstanding examples of Romanesque architecture in the world.

H.V. Morton described it as the most remarkable he had ever seen. He describes it as having been built by the Normans -apparently with a chisel in one hand and a sword in the other! He describes it as the only piece of gay (not today's meaning) Norman architecture he has ever seen. He called it Norman architecture with a sense of humour.

The explanation, he found more remarkable still. It is the only great piece of Norman architecture in the British Isles that was not built by the Normans themselves! It was built fifty years before Strongbow made his first landing.

Cashel remains the visible link with the Gaelic Ireland which, subject to invasion and oppression has stubbornly survived: the Ireland of the Book of Kells, the Cross of Cong and the Tara Brooch.

St. Patrick is said to have visited here in 450AD and there is a cross with a carving of him on it.

This imposing edifice, so steeped in religious history is reputed to have been planted by the devil himself! The story goes that as the devil was flying home (to England, of course) across the plain of Tipperary, he took a savage bite out of the northern hills in passing, but dropped the rocky mouthful in the centre of the Golden Vale. It is a fact that when you look in the right direction, toward the Slieve-Bloom Mountains, you can see the gap in the remote hills which Cashel, it seems, would exactly fit. They call it the Devil's Bit, (or should it be, 'bite'?)

'Time', in Ireland seems an irrelevance. They can talk about the past as yesterday or the day before. It matters not. Here in Cashel they still talk about the baptism of King Aengus as if it had just happened.

The King was baptized by St. Patrick, who was by then, old and feeble, on the ancient coronation stone of the high Kings of Cashel. In order to support himself he drove the spiked point of his crozier into the ground. When the ceremony was over, blood was left on the grass. It appears, the crozier had pierced the foot of the King. St. Patrick asked the King why he had not cried out in pain. The King replied that he had heard so much about the sufferings of our Lord that he was proud to bear the agony.

It was early evening when I left Cashel. The sun had just set but the air was still pleasantly warm and comforting. A bright yellow moon, in all its fulness turned the Plain of Tipperary into a world of silver. I thought of that wonderful poem of Walter De La Mare -
'Softly, silently, now the moon walks the night in her silvery shoon'.
I wished I could do the same and capture the scene for immortality.

I took one last lingering look at the Rock. It stood there as if carved out of silver ... magnificent!

XXXI

It was late evening when I entered Thomastown: too late for Kilkenny. The little town was deserted and dark. I way-laid a stray old man taking his dog for a walk. He directed me to BallyDuff House, a former 18th Century manor house, now an hotel. It was set back, over-looking the river, which he told me, with pride, was teeming with salmon and trout.

It was quite a luxurious place, with spacious bedrooms overlooking the wide, open, countryside. The catering too was in keeping with the comfort.

I was delighted to find my favourite dish on the menu - cooked mussels marinated in a white wine sauce.
I am not a gourmet by any means and, like my father before me maintain, 'I eat to live, not live to eat!'

Food, is not my priority but in the case of 'mussels' I do acknowledge their attraction. With a little vinegar-dip handy and some warm, crisp bread, I have a feast.

Thomastown in daylight is not exactly impressive but it has a cosiness about it that spells 'self-satisfaction'. It has not altered since I was last here in 1992, or I suspect, since HVMorton's visit.

Among my many Irish relatives I unearthed a cousin who lived deep in the countryside a few miles outside of Thomastown. She informed me it would be impossible to direct me to their little estate so, she would come and fetch me.

Following her in her Range-Rover down winding, high, leafy lanes was tantamount to finding oneself in the maze at Hampton Court Palace. Eventually we reached a collection of four or five substantial houses set in their own spacious grounds, on a hillside looking down into a golden vale, I could only marvel at the beauty of this world.

There would be some that would consider themselves cut off from life but here is the very essence of life itself. The houses themselves have every modern convenience; Thomastown is the nearest place to buy provisions while Kilkenny on a market -day is but a short drive further on. My first thoughts are 'Heaven'. She has been here for thirty years and is well content.

Their little estate of several acres is well-stocked with orchards and vegetable garden. Nor is the aesthetic side neglected. The ornate flower-gardens are alive with every bloom and plant conceivable. All this, she has built up from the empty land they bought so cheaply, years ago. I am humbled!

Being a member of the Butler clan is still something of importance in Kilkenny and they were anxious to take me to the castle to see 'our ancestors', as it were. I had missed visiting it in 1992 but I can recall HV's comments.

He made little comment on its appearance beyond saying it was as feudal-looking as any he had seen and that it contained many pictures and the signature of every King of England since Henry 11.
The pictures he referred to would have been the portraits of the Butlers from earliest times to the latest. I looked for any, even the slightest sign of family resemblance; our wishful thinking brought many, 'Ah, yes's,' along with the other thousands of 'would be' descendants. It was all very innocuous and amusing.

The castle, the strong-hold of the Butlers, Dukes of Ormonde and the most powerful in Ireland, dates back to the 1100s was built by Theobald Fitzwalter, chief Butler of Ireland. His family took the name Butler and as Earls and Dukes of Ormonde lived in the castle until 1935.

Kilkenny town can be very interesting and a good starting point, as in many other places, is the Tourist Information Centre in Rose Inn Street.

The centre occupies the Shee Alms House, an old Tudor Alms House. Here you can watch a video presentation of Kilkenny's history. Just around the corner is the arcaded Tholsel, built in 1761 of black Kilkenny marble as a Toll-House and now serving as the Town Hall. The road then runs on to Parliament Street through the heart of medieval Kilkenny with little alleyways running in all directions off it.

At the northern end of the main street is St. Cornice's Cathedral. This was of particular interest to me as inside was a collection of tombs and monuments dating as far back as 1285, with many of them commemorating members of the Butler family of Kilkenny Castle. The cathedral, situated in the old Irish Town district recalls the past segregation of the town. The area still known as English Town still has the finest buildings.

H.V.Morton –
'It was in Kilkenny Castle that Parliament was summoned by Vice-Roy, Lionel, Duke of Clarence, in 1367, when the Statute of Kilkenny was called. The object of the Act was to separate the two races, Irish and English. 'The Irish enemies,' as they were called and the 'Degenerate English'.

Its main points were:
'Alliance with the Irish by marriage, fosterage, and gossipred (god-parents) were forbidden as high treason and punishable by death. Any Englishman, by birth or blood who took an Irish name, spoke the Irish language, wore the Irish dress, or adopted any Irish custom should forfeit his estates.
No Englishman was to allow the Irish to graze cattle on his land, to grant livings to Irish clergy, or to entertain the Irish Bards, pipers or story-tellers.'

The streets of Kilkenny are old-fashioned and rather grim but its long main street has some fine Georgian Buildings.
The main landmark on the High Street is the 18th Century Tholsel with its clock-tower and arcade.

One thing I like about these Irish towns is their abundance of individually owned little shops. Most of them are painted in the old brown and green. The window-dressing too is delightfully archaic and amateurish. It reminds me much of England before the war. The only concession to a large Super-Store is Dunnes.

There are parks and recreation centres and on the whole seems a pleasant, old-fashioned place with a rooted community and an air of quiet permanence.

I couldn't leave Kilkenny until I had heard their version of 'The Kilkenny Cats'. The Information Centre had all the answers.
'In the old days' she told me, 'Kilkenny had two towns. Irish Town and English Town. There was continual feuding between them. You could say, they fought like cats. Then, there is another story. When Cromwell was here, his troopers, to amuse themselves, would tie two cats together by their tails, then tie a rope across the road , sling the cats over it and watch them fight.

When Cromwell heard of it he forbid any such antics. The Irish version goes on;
As two officers were seen approaching, there was no time to separate the cats so they just cut off their tails and told the officers that they had fought till nothing was left.'

I stayed the night in another B&B bungalow. Breakfast was served on the terrace.

There was not another house in sight. The expanse of green fields stretched to a bordering woodland, with a winding river threading its way through, it was truly enchanting.

I am told they paid £500 for the land and built the house themselves. I met a couple from Paris. We had language problems but managed to communicate in spite of them and talked about religion, language and history.

XXXII

I am heading now for Carlow. This is still 'Horsey Country' as HV Morton called it. It is the home of the thorough-bred horse industry. Here is the famous Curragh, a grassy plain in County Kildare, like Salisbury Plain in England. Here is the Irish National Stud where the finest race-horses in the world are bred.
A notice in a Kildare shop told me a race-meeting was on; I decided to go.

The race-course, the home of the Irish Derby, is deserted but the plain is dotted with race-horses at exercise. The meeting is well -attended. In the packed Grand-Stand I feel I am surrounded by the most knowledgeable 'horseymen' in the world. They live and breathe 'horses'.

I don't know what to say about Carlow. It is undeniable pretty and attractive, too much so! It is not Irish! It is more like a 'chocolate-box' village in England. The immaculate, thatched, white-washed cottages, with old men in the garden, pottering about or just sat, watching the world go by.

XXXIII

I take the N9 on my way to Glendalough. When I reach Timolin I turn off and take the A147 to Baltinglass. Back on the N81 to Holywood, where stands the very fine Hastings Culloden House Hotel. It was originally the palace for the Bishops of Down and retains much of its former opulence.

The A76 winds its way over the Wicklow Mountains. When HV Morton came down this road he commented on what he called, 'the incense of Ireland, the smell of turf-fires from the one -storey, stone, white-washed cabins, so white they hurt the eyes as they sit there in the dazzling sun'.

The cabins are gone and so has most of the 'incense'. The smart modern bungalows with their central-heating have replaced them. No longer do we see the farmer's wife leading her little donkey and cart to the next market town.

Today, the modern white houses and bungalows may have replaced the cabins but the long winding roads and the stone walls are still here, imprisoning as it were, this half-magical fairy-land of a country.
And so I came to Glendalough. One cannot think of Glendalough without the name of St. Kevin coming up. He was the founder of Glendalough. The story says he came here from England in the year 520, when surely there were few Christians. He came, it says, to lead a hermit's life.

He met the beautiful Kathleen, the source of a thousand songs and poems who favoured him with her ardour. Kevin rejected her allure and he was driven into solitude. The tale continues that one day, finding the young monk alone in the fields, she embraced him passionately but he resisted her charms and grabbing a handful of nettles struck her with them until, blistered, her love for him shrank. An alternative idea is that he just pushed her into the lake.

He made himself a retreat in the hollow of a tree then later, in a cave, high up the mountain.

Disciples came until it was a little sanctuary of holy-men. St. Kevin sent his disciples to found schools and monasteries in other parts of Ireland.

I think of Lindisfarne and St. Cuthbert and Glastonbury and Joseph of Aramathea but think no place has given me a clearer picture of early Christianity than Glendalough.

This is a heavenly little valley with its two small lakes cupped in a hollow in the hills. The hills are high and the lakes so deep that even on a sunny day the waters are still and black.

By the side of the lake stands one of those refuge towers built a thousand years ago to escape marauding Danes and Vikings.

It is a sober thought to ponder, that when the sound of sword upon sword and bloody conflict was to be heard in England, here in Glendalough, the bells rang for Mass.
The boatman that took me over the lake, was, like all Irishmen, full of stories. It seems they have all kissed the Blarney Stone.

I asked him if he thought it was true that St. Kevin had pushed Kathleen in the lake.

'They all ask me that,' he replied.
'No kind of Saint would do that. The truth is that after he had bothered her with the nettles she was cured of her love and became a nun.'

I asked him how deep he thought the lake actually was. I should have known better as he pursed up his mouth and looked solemn. He gave me the stock reply he told all his listeners.

'It's that deep sir, that my sister came bathing here and she sank.'
He paused and looked gravely at me, without a glimmer of a twinkle in his eye.

'We heard not a word from her until we got a letter from Manchester asking us to post her some dry clothes. That's how deep it is sir.'

He was doing his job well!

The settlement was sacked time and time again by the Vikings but nevertheless flourished for 600 years but decline set in after the English forces razed the site in 1398 although it continued as a monastic centre until the dissolution of the monasteries by Henry V111 in 1549. However pilgrims still come to Glendalough, especially on June 3rd. St. Kevin's Feast Day.

XXXIV

They sing of the rocky road to Dublin. If the road itself is not so rocky, as when the song was written, the route through the rugged wilderness of the Wicklow Mountains is still as wild as ever.

The mountains once provided a safe hide-out from enemies. When much of the Southeast was obedient to English rule, the area around Dublin, known as 'The Pale' was where war-lords such as the O'Tooles held sway in the mountains.

Here too, in the 1798 uprising, the rebels sought refuge. In 1803 a military road around Sally Gap was made and the area lost much of its age-long security.
The scenery is still exhilarating with its rock-strewn glens, lush forests and bog-land and purple-sheen heather. Turf-cutting is still a thriving cottage industry and stacks of peat lie alongside the road and overall hangs that distinctive, uniquely Irish, ambient smell of burning peat, or, in HVMorton's words :
'I smell for the first time, the incense of Ireland, the smoke of turf fires.'

As I near Dublin, I come to the Powerscourt Estate to pay a visit to the famous gardens. Powerscourt House has been re-built after being destroyed by fire in 1974. The deer-park with its Japanese Sika deer and their distinctive white rumps was created by Lord Powerscourt in the 1760's. It was the painting by George Barret of the waterfall, over 400 feet, the highest in all Ireland, that brought tourists. The Dargle Valley below the falls is rich in wild life, with oak trees, redwoods, beech, birch and rowan, forming a habitat for many birds.

I see a sign… 'Sally Gap'. I ponder, why does Ireland have such unusual names for perfectly ordinary things? The road now starts to climb through partly reforested hills. At the top of the rise you reach Sally Gap and cross the old military road that was built through the Wicklows around 1800.

I am nearing the outskirts of Dublin now. I recall a visit I paid in 1947 when I met an old ex Lord Mayor of the city, Alfie Byrne, who took me on a conducted tour of the Da'il Eireanne, which is of course, the Parliament of the Irish Republic. It was formerly the residence of the Dukes of Leinster. When I told him my Uncle Barney owned the Gaiety Theatre, he was over-joyed and said he knew him well. His portrait used to line the wall in the entrance foyer. I wonder if it is still there. He lived in a grand house at Black-Rock. He made his money touring in a comedy duo, 'Armstrong and Kelly'. At one time he owned several small cinemas in the country but lost a lot in the 'troubles' after the 1916 rebellion or so the story goes. But in Ireland it is difficult to relate fact from fiction. I was pleasantly surprised to learn from Alfie that there was some substance in the tales.

Terenure is a suburb of Dublin. There are some substantial 'middle-class' dwellings of the late 19th and early 20th century. It looks like many of them, having fallen on hard times, have become B&B houses. As I move on, the standard of households becomes more 'working-class' terrace-type.

I am told by a resident that it is not safe to leave a car parked in Dublin: better to go in by bus. I settle for what seems a decent B&B and catch a bus into Dublin.

I get off at College Green, do a tour of the college. The young under-graduate was very knowledgeable and pointed out the different styles of architecture, including the 1960s library which I thought reminded me of a concrete bunker!

I was anxious to set eyes on the most precious book in existence... 'The Book of Kells'. This book is taken from its case every evening and locked in a safe in the vaults; every morning it is carried back to its glass case again and one leaf is turned each day. The book is priceless and yet it is not insured! It is thought, 'no money in the world could produce another such book so the best insurance is to spend money on extra fire-precautions'.

Dublin boasts three Cathedrals. One of them is Christ Church Cathedral. It is very old. The crypt is said to have been built when Sigtrygg Silkbeard was King of Dublin.

When this crypt was built there were men alive who remembered the battle of Clontarf. There is a glass case in which can be seen the mummified forms of a cat and a rat. Both animals seem to have died in life-like positions: the cat springing after the rat and the rat in full flight from the cat. The story goes that the cat followed the rat into an organ pipe, which became their tomb...

Christ Church was built twenty years after the battle of Clontarf. Between that time and the building of the crypt the Kingdom of Ireland relapsed again into petty states and Irish history becomes lost in a mist until the long boats of the Vikings beached on the east coast of Ireland and founded the little settlement on Dublin Bay.

Here, in Christ Church is the tomb of Strongbow, the founder of all Ireland's troubles. He held Dublin for Henry 11.

The stories of his ruthlessness linger on to this day. There is a small stone effigy that lay beside his tomb. It is of a young man but it is cut off at the waist. It is the son of Strongbow, who, because he had shown cowardice in battle, was killed by his father and then cut in two as a warning to all cowards.

Near-by is the Protestant St. Patrick's Cathedral. Here you will find the graves of Swift and Stella together at last in death. An epitaph, that no one but Swift could have written runs thus:
'Here lies the body of Jonathan Swift,
For thirty years dean of this cathedral
Where savage indignation can
No longer gnaw his heart-
Go, traveller, and
Imitate, if you can, one who
Played a man's part in defence
Of Liberty'

These words have gone round the world.

Other things to be seen in St. Patrick's are, the flags of disbanded Irish regiments, and the stall of the knights of St. Patrick and other memorials but always one returns to the two stones in the nave which cover the bodies of the two most mysterious lovers in English literature.

I headed for the Gaiety Theatre to see if there was any trace left of Uncle Barney. I was disappointed: not only that but no one could even recall him ...Ah well.

It seemed a long walk to the Guinness Brewery but I was determined to see the home of this world-famous brew.

These days - 2009, visitors can only visit the Hop-House - a kind of museum of the history of Guinness. This is a poor substitution for the original tour I did in 1947. These tours ended in 1972 - what a pity! I well remember the 1947 visit, where, after several hours seeing the nectar going through all its processes, was conducted to a tiny 'snug' where a fairly large silver tankard of Guinness was given to me to imbibe. It was fairly weak stuff---X, I believe. After that it was filled, or perhaps, half-filled, with XX. It was a good drink but I was not allowed to finish ...yet. XXX came next; you could float a spoon in it. Then to finish off...some XXXX for export. Don't remember what I thought of it but I can remember feeling very bloated and light-headed and vaguely thinking this was not a very wise thing to do, unless they could lead you to a cosy bed to sleep it off. However, being 1947 and Ireland being neutral, they were not rationed as we were in England, so I ordered grilled ham with 'two' eggs and ate myself into some sobriety.

This mild, vacuous tour today did not lend itself to any such-like adventure.

My 1947 tour of the brewery entailed all the processes to manufacture this 'liquid gold'.

First, the ground malt was mashed in water in copper kieves - man-sized saucepans with lids. The malt came from silvery hoppers overhead and was mixed with roasted barley to give the stout a dark colour. During the mash the starch turned into a kind of sugar The liquid was then drained from the mash which was then called, 'Wort' and was pumped into coppers, each holding 24,000 gallons and boiled with hops.

Through the windows I could see the dark liquid boiling furiously. Next, the 'wort' was strained off and pumped into huge aluminium chambers. I could see the foam working away as alcohol and carbonic gas was thrown up. The yeast was then skimmed off and the stout went into vats along the mains of the tunnel and into casks or tankers ready for delivery to 'the world'.

Legend has it that Guinness brewed with water from the Liffey is 'the best.' Looking at those murky waters does not inspire one as to its truth and it is best to leave the legend to the romantics.

Without a doubt, the finest street in Dublin is O' Connell Street.
The G.P.O. stands there, restored after its battering by the British Army in the 1916 rebellion.

Events then took a turn from which there was no 'coming-back'.
250,000 Irishmen were, at that time, fighting alongside the British in the great World War raging in France.

Irish Independence had been put aside but not forgotten.
Extreme nationalists, - impatient, saw an opportunity to seize power.

When war broke out in Europe, in 1914, both Carson and Redmond, the leaders of the main parties, called for support for Britain. Their call was answered and 200,000 volunteers enlisted in the British Army. 60,000 never returned.

In spite of this, nowhere in the Republic will you find a memorial to those who died ...sad.

The war brought prosperity to Ireland and agricultural prices rose as Britain turned to Ireland for food supplies. Employment increased and the country was peaceful and doing well.

There was, however, a movement headed by Eoion Mc.Neil who refused to follow Redmond's lead and kept themselves armed to enforce Britain's promise of Home-Rule after the war. The most extreme of this 16,000 strong movement wanted to take advantage of Britain's plight and have a rebellion while the war was on. The rebels sought aid from Germany and that country responded by sending a ship, The Aud, with guns. The rebellion was planned for Easter Sunday, 1916, when the guns were due.

McNeil, the leader of the volunteers did not favour a rebellion, thinking it would not only fail but the people were against it.

But when he was shown a document (now thought perhaps forged) authorizing the arrest of the leaders, he gave the order to rise, but on Good Friday, the British Navy captured the German gun ship and the spy who had co-ordinated the plot, Sir Roger Casement, was captured when he returned from Germany. Plans were thrown askew but they decided to make a desperate attempt on Bank Holiday Monday.

A bewildered holiday crowd of civilians watched as the volunteers marched down O'Connell Street to take over the G.P.O. as their headquarters. The Irish Tricolour was run up and Pearse read the proclamation to an indifferent crowd. Several other buildings were taken over by other leaders, among them was Eamon de Valera.

Britain responded by sending a gunboat, the Helga, into Dublin Bay. It shelled O'Connell Street and Pearse, outnumbered, surrendered.

The immediate reaction of the people, especially in Dublin, was one of anger where jobs had been destroyed and lives endangered. Five hundred and fifty people had been killed and two thousand injured besides nearly £3 million worth of damage.

The British Army, under Sir John Maxwell was given a free hand. He retaliated by taking prisoner thousands of people and sending them to prison camps in England.

The leaders were tried and fifteen men were sentenced to be shot.

The previously, largely indifferent civilian population, hearing rumours of atrocities began to turn its sympathy towards the rebels.

Shooting them was the biggest mistake made by the British government. The poet, W.B.Yeats, expressed the new attitude in the lines:
I write it out in a verse,
McDonagh and McBride
And Connolly and Pearse
Now and in time to be

Wherever green is worn
Are changed, changed utterly,
A terrible beauty is born.

The dead men had taken their places alongside Tone and Emmet among the heroes of nationalist Ireland.

In 1917, the various groups that opposed British rule came together under de Valera. A final blow at conciliation with the British came when, in 1918, conscription was brought in. This move united the Irish as never before. The British were forced to withdraw it and Sinn Fein was given the credit for its removal.

I sometimes think that every Irishman has kissed the Blarney Stone, for conversation seems to come so effortlessly, then I think it would be a superfluous act because they all seem blessed with this 'gift of the gab' as a natural inheritance.

I remember once, talking to a man I met in a café in O'Connell Street. Someone had blown up Nelson's Column and the debris was now being cleared. He evidently surmised this was taking up my thoughts, for without so much as an introduction, he broke in with:
"Ah! Poor old Nelson, what a shame."
I turned to him in surprise. His tone was so intimate and friendly sympathetic that it immediately sent warning bells ringing in my head.
"An Irishman lamenting over Nelson? I couldn't believe it!"
He continued in this vein, taking great pains to express his admiration of all things British and regretting the division that had occurred between us. It was all 'over the top'.
It was a pity. I should have liked to believe him.

He told me, in confidence, that in 1972 it was planned for the Irish Army to invade Northern Ireland and establish a united country. I like an argument but I was unable to take the conversation further and just let him drool on. We parted on amicable terms.

Ireland has done well through the European Union; it has received more Euros per capita than any other member. This has resulted in a higher standard of living than the U.K. and stemmed their emigration problem. Ireland now has a population of about four million: 40% of it under twenty five. It is strange and sad to think that less than two hundred years ago it had double that.

Close by The Viking Centre, similar to the 'Jorvik Centre' at York, is Temple Bar...a must for visitors.

At Temple Bar you can sample contemporary Irish arts and culture. Here, in a spectacular open-air performance area, are, the gallery of photography, The Irish Film Centre, The Temple Bar Music Centre, 'Arthouse', a multi-media centre for the arts, The Ark, a cultural centre for children, and every Saturday, The Book Market provides a gathering place for independent book-sellers.

In a contemplative mood my meanderings brought me to Dublin Castle. The original castle was built for King John in 1207. The only remaining structure is the massive stone Record Tower. The Great Courtyard is surrounded by a medley of attractive buildings. The State Apartments, built for the English Vice-Roy and now the venue for Ireland's Presidencies of the European Community.

There may be many more cities, larger and grander than Dublin but none can equal it in its infinite varieties of interest. Every mundane little street contains its own unique item of interest.

I found myself walking down a row of neat little houses, recently lovingly restored to something of their Victorian appearance. It is Synge Street and at number 33 I stop and pause. The great Irish playwright, George Bernard Shaw was born here in 1856 and spent his early years. I try to see beyond the spotless white lace curtains and see the family at home, all those years ago. I go inside and find myself in a typical middle-class Victorian home looking very much as it was then. Any minute I expect the family to return.

Ireland is rightly proud of its contribution to literature and in Parnell Square is the Dublin Writers' Museum. It is a fine 18th century mansion that now houses the works and lives of Swift, Sheridan, Shaw, Wilde, Yeats, Joyce and Beckett. I think it nothing short of a miracle that out of this tiny grief stricken island throughout all its traumatic history, such a collection of genius has manifested itself.

131

A little further on in N. Gt George's St. is the James Joyce Centre a museum dedicated to promoting interest in the life works of James Joyce.

Here is another interesting paradox. Joyce was not the most widely read author. Indeed, outside academic circles it is difficult to find anyone who has read any of his controversial works. And yet, now, he stands like a colossus in world literature. It's a strange world.

I cross over the Liffey and a short walk eastwards from the O'Connell Bridge brings me to the world famous Abbey Theatre. This was founded in 1904 by Lady Gregory, W.B. Yeats and J.M.Synge.

It has premiered the works of every leading Irish playwright. In 1951 it was destroyed by fire and the brutalist building that now replaces it has two theatres, The Abbey, which is devoted to the Irish classics and the Peacock which specialises in experimental drama.

Phoenix Park lies a mile or so to the west of The Four Courts, the seat of Justice in Ireland. The huge area of land about the size of Hyde Park, serves as a lung to the city.

In 1640, these former Priory lands were seized and turned into a royal deer park. Later, a Vice-Roy's residence was built here and it is now the official residence of the Irish President.

It is impossible to miss the towering Wellington Memorial, 205 feet high, in honour of the victor of Waterloo, Arthur Wellesley. The Iron Duke, was never proud of his Irish origins and is forever remembered for his disparaging remark:

'Being born in a stable doesn't make one a horse'.

I claimed Dublin a city of interest without peer and to further my claim I go no further than St. Michan's Church.

At first glance, there is nothing about St. Michan's to tempt one to even cast a glance at it. It is an unpretentious, ancient church, said to have been founded by a Danish Bishop in 1095 A.D. It was re-built on town-hall lines in the 18th century. It was built on the site of an old oak forest and herein lies its uniqueness for as soon as you descend into the vaults below, you notice the air is not like the chilled clammy air you expect: it is almost warm and of a surprising freshness.

'This', says the Sexton, 'is the best air in Dublin'.

The thought flashes through my mercenary mind...

'I'm surprised you haven't tried to bottle it and make it another Irish Guinness.'

But, what visitors go to St. Michan's for, is not the bracing air. They are lured by a more sinister, morbid curiosity. They go to see the mummies! Mummies as perfectly preserved as those so carefully preserved by the Pharaohs.

The difference is, no man-made artifice has been used to keep them so preserved. H.V.Morton writes –

'In the vaults, a number of high-vaulted cells lead off from each side of a central passage running east and west beneath the church. They are fitted with iron gates. The sexton takes a torch, opens a gate, and, leading the way into one of the vaults, flashes his torch over the most ghastly sight you can imagine.

Coffins lay stacked one upon another, almost to the roof. You are in the vault of a noble family. Lords and ladies, generals and statesmen, known and unknown, lie around you. The last coffin placed in position rests on others, which in their turn rest on that of their great great-grandfather. The lower coffins are of a shape and colour long out-dated. Some, which bear coats of arms are covered in red velvet, which has not decayed much or faded in colour; others are bound in black leather, and are studded with big brass nails which have not tarnished.

When you look more closely you notice that the weight of the dead pressing on the dead has caused the coffins to collapse into one another, exposing here a hand, there an arm, a leg or a head.'

The very thought of dead men pushing their ancestors from their coffins is worthy of any supernatural thriller novel.

The startling fact is that these men and women, many of whom have been dead 500 years have not gone back to dust; they are like mummies, their flesh is the texture of tough leather, and stranger still, their joints work.

The Sexton pointed out to me, as to HVM, that 'the body of a man lying with one leg crossed over the other, the traditional death posture of a Crusader. This indicated that he had been to the Holy Land.' I have seen this position many times before captured on stone tombs but never a crusader himself.

'You can shake hands with him,' said the Sexton. I bent down and examined the finger nails of a man who died 800 years ago.

In another vault is the body of a woman, said to be a nun, whose feet and right hand have been amputated. The story is that she was tortured and mutilated hundreds of years ago.'

We went into many other vaults. In one, there were fragments of this family lying about all over the floor in the thin grey dust of decayed coffins. It was a veritable nightmare!

Not everything was dead! When I first visited the place, it was the home of a unique collection of spiders! Learned men from all over the world come here. There was an unrivalled variety of the creatures here.
'But what did they feed on?' I asked, dreading the answer. He laughed as he read my thoughts.
'Themselves; they're cannibals.'

I remember asking:
'What's the answer to all this then?'
The generally accepted one is that the air in the vaults is chemically impregnated by the remains of the oak forest which stood here in ancient times. So long as the vaults are kept perfectly dry, decay ceases. If only a little moisture enters, then the bodies and coffins crumble into fine dust. For instance, when the two brothers, John and Henry Shears, who were beheaded in the 18th century, were re-coffined in 1853 - they used to stand upright in a vault with their heads beside their feet - the people of

Dublin brought wreaths and flowers to the vault. The moisture in these flowers wrecked everything in the vault within a year.'

St. Michan's is like a real world Madame Tussaud's chamber of horrors.

I was glad to get back into the real world of light and sunshine.

Dublin is not merely a tourist city; it is a homely city. One has not long to be here before you find yourself saying:
"I could live here."
And indeed I could. On the one hand you have a city that offers everything of interest and entertainment. There are rich residential suburbs all within striking distance of the centre, offering magnificent Victorian mansions as well as the most modern of houses. Surrounding the city are expanses of wild moorland comparable with those of the Derbyshire Peak District. It is not just that a Dublin man can shoot grouse on the hills within six miles of the G.P.O. or he can grass trout as easily, it is more than that! It is the Irish themselves. They are not as formal, or as stuffy as we are, what matters to them is 'talk' and 'laughter'. Their hospitality is abounding. But while there is no limit to their welcome there is nothing more devastating than their disapproval. For throughout Irish life and conversation there runs a bitterness that eventually one accepts. The charm of Irish conversation is that it is undisciplined. It is a riot of good things. Irish thought and expression are simultaneous. Put all these together and you have Dublin. It is perhaps strange that one cannot honestly call Dublin a typical Irish city. It is more a relic of a grand Anglo/ Norman/Viking/ Georgian city. There is nowhere quite like it!
Before I left Dublin, I was shown an Irish Language Menu. Even before I read it, I thought,
'Well, whatever it is, how delicious it may sound, no one will be able to match its progression from the Irish kitchen to the Irish stomach.' 'It read:
'Starters....'French-fried semi-colon in marinated white wine.
Sirloin Snake stuffed with infinitives. Saddle of mule, with or without stirrup. Ragout de Cheval Et Lupin. (Horse Rabbit Stew) washed down with 'Tipperary Tumble' Vintage 1916.
All served with full Irish humour.'

I left Dublin with some reluctance, knowing I had only tapped into its many attractions, but, as always, 'time is of the essence' and among other things, I was anxious to explore the land of 'The Brontes'.

5.30pm and the rush home had started. I found a Typical Irish Restaurant; ordered a typical Irish tea of thick, grilled Irish ham, two eggs, pineapple (new since the Yanks introduced it), toast, best Irish butter, fruit salad, glass of grapefruit juice, large pot of tea, and 'Bob's m'uncle', or 'Queen's m'auntie'. A pleasant way to spend the next couple of hours till the rush was over.

XXXV

A few miles north of the city on the R105, I run into the suburb of Marino. It was here, in the 1750's that Lord Charlemont built a summer residence. It was rescued from decay and neglect and restored to its former magnificence in 1984.

Drogheda is where I am heading and on the way I pass through the delightful little resorts of Balbriggan and Skerries but I have no time to linger and reached Drogheda about 8pm.

It is not an inspiring sight! I noticed a Martello tower and the bleak remains of an old castle but the general aspect did not look attractive enough to warrant a stay of any length.

I thought of the Siege of Drogheda and decided that I must first find a place for the night and explore the town the next day. I found a very comfortable B&B a few miles north of Drogheda. The landlord, a youngish man of thirty five or so was very hospitable and helpful. He showed me several books of local interest and waxed enthusiastic on what he called: 'The oldest building in the world' at Newgrange. He also revealed some interesting facts about the Battle of Boyne and other snippets of local history regarding Drogheda. He was an Irish patriot and his covert politeness and amiability did not disguise his antipathy towards the English and their occupation in N.Ireland. He believed, unequivocally, in a united Ireland and nothing less. Once again there arose the startling revelation that in 1972, plans were made for a military intervention by the Republic to seize back, by force, the six counties of N. Ireland!

The next morning I drove back the few miles into Drogheda down long, winding country lanes, through remote little villages, very much of a sameness. For mile after mile there is nothing but flat fields and hedges: unlike England with its great urban spread, that is swallowing up the countryside.

'This', I thought, 'is what England was like before the industrial revolution.'

It is a wet, windy, bleak morning, and a cold grey sky hangs overhead: a seemingly solid mass without a break in the clouds. The rain is falling in a steady monotonous downpour. But it is Irish rain: soft and gentle.

It was still raining when I reached Drogheda. It is perhaps unfair to judge anywhere on a dull, dreary day. It may give one a more honest and realistic assessment but it is akin to seeing a glamorous film star without her 'make-up'.

After twelve hours of rain, Drogheda is almost awash. The narrow streets with their never-ending streams of traffic, splashing pedestrians, adding to the torment of battling their way through the crowds, half the time with one foot in the gutter.

The shops, by English standards were dowdy and old fashioned, as if one had stepped back into the 1930s. It is only when a modern Super-Market appears do you realise it is 2009.

The Super or Hyper Market has not yet destroyed Ireland. Ireland still retains its own, individual, Irish named shops and this is what makes it different and so attractive. Much of what the tourist has come to see is derived from the cinema. There are disappointments, such as 'The Claddagh' and all the Irish don't live in picturesque cabins, like John Wayne, in 'The Quiet Man'. Things have moved on from 'Man of Arran'.

Drogheda was a miserable experience. I sought refuge in the Tourist Information Centre. It was warm and cosy. It appeared there was a lot to see in Drogheda. The lady in attendance was charming and helpful.

'Where are you from?' she asked.
'England,' I answered.
For a second, the smiling face froze, then she recovered and added, rather patronisingly:
'Never mind, you're welcome, just the same.'

I didn't know what to make of the remark. Was she being condescending, sympathetic, diplomatic or what?

I thanked her for her help and as I left, I turned and stopped in the doorway.
'By the way,' I said 'have you heard? ...Cromwell's dead!'
I stayed not for an answer but slid quietly out.

When I read Antonia Fraser's biography of Cromwell, 'Our Chief of Men', knowing she was a Catholic, I felt how fair and balanced, neither biased nor prejudiced was her assessment of the Siege of Drogheda. It could easily have been otherwise.

It may have been of less importance than the Battle of the Boyne but it was more terrible and left Cromwell as the most hated man in Ireland and even wider, the Catholic world. Even so, Antonia Fraser was magnanimous enough to call him, 'Strict but fair.' She conceded he saw Ireland as a Holy War. He was prejudiced by the religious and nationalistic attitude of his time. He had friends who had suffered at the hands of the rebels and he himself, had invested money in Ireland in the form of loans that would one day be paid back in Irish land.

He saw the invasion as a crusade, perhaps settled by a settlement of godly people who would give the ancient name of Ireland,' the island of the Saints', a very different meaning.

Cromwell invaded Ireland with a formidable armada of thirty five ships, followed by Treton, with another seventy seven. It was a Protestant crusade against the barbarous and bloodthirsty Irish. Clearly, Cromwell saw himself as bringing the Gospel of Christ and establishing truth and peace.

As Antonia Fraser, in her book, put it:
'The combination of religious proselytising zeal with future financial profit, was a heady one.'

Cromwell believed he was crusading against a 'priest-ridden', drunken, barbarous, vicious bunch of men. This was the mood before he commenced his Siege of Drogheda.

Although he had vastly superior forces at his disposal, he hoped to take the town by peaceful methods. He was encouraged in this by large numbers of men that deserted from the Irish army to join his own.

He offered his first summons to surrender to the town to secure its obedience and avoid bloodshed.

At that time the rules of war were very clear:
If a Commander refused to accede to a summons to surrender and force had to be used, he then put at risk, the lives not only of his own men but of all those who could be held to be combatants.

The defendants knew a siege could be very wasteful; men sitting endlessly before a fortress became susceptible to disease; supplies could run out and the men could be debilitated in every sense. Add to that their growing annoyance and dissatisfactions at being kept from their homes, unnecessarily longer than needs be.

Cromwell was aware that his troops were already suffering from exposure, lying there in their wet tents.

It was therefore a good move if a besieged commander could hold out as long as possible, unless he had an incentive to surrender.

There were strict rules to be followed once the walls were breached:
'No quarter was to be given!'
By surrendering, lives would be saved and the sieges shorter.

The Irish Commander of Drogheda responded by declaring he would rather perish than surrender. This meant the civilian population could not be protected.

Cromwell's first attack was repelled. The walls were pounded by his artillery and a breach was made. An offer of quarter was made and rejected. Cromwell in his fury then ordered 'no quarter' and his troops ran riot. Blood-lust swept through the Protestant forces unchecked. Over a thousand people died in the onslaught; friars and priests were treated as combatants and they too were slaughtered to a man. Prisoners were taken and sent as slaves to the plantations in Barbados.

After the siege, Cromwell wrote;

'I am persuaded that this was a righteous judgement of God upon these barbarous wretches who have embraced their hands in so much innocent blood!'

Time heals but this is Ireland and it could have been last week!

It was in a somewhat sombre mood I moved on.

XXXVI

I remembered the enthusiasm of the young man when he spoke of Newgrange, so I headed west from Drogheda through lush fields and pastures so like the English countryside.

Newgrange, I was told, was over a thousand years before Stonehenge when Ireland was truly a Celtic country. It is a Neolithic monument where, according to Celtic lore, the legendary Kings of Tara were buried but archaeologists predates them and estimates it was built around 3000BC.

Whoever it was, they clearly had exceptional artistic and engineering skills.
There were about 200,000 tonnes transported to the mound or cairn which protects the passage grave. Larger slabs were used to make the circle around the cairn, the kerb and the tomb itself. Many of the kerb stones and the slabs lining the passage, the chamber and its recesses are decorated with zig-zags, spirals and other geometric motifs. The grave's corbelled ceiling consists of smaller, unadorned slabs and has proved completely water-proof for the last 5000 years.

Many theories and hypotheses have been put forward. One that seems logical is the association with Time.

Every year, at dawn on the 21st December, at exactly two minutes to nine a shaft of sunlight beams through the roof-box and travels along the nineteen metres passage and hits the central recess in the burial chamber of the dead.

It stops that way for exactly seventeen minutes.

The guide went on to relate another half-dozen theories. As he said, 'You takes your pick.'

It was about 1pm when I emerged from this unique place. It had stopped raining and the surrounding rich countryside looked gloriously alive with its rich pastures and its sea of golden corn waving gently in the warm summer breeze. What a contrast to the cold monument of death I had just left.

There is a sense of mystery and spirituality around this part of Ireland and I think of Tara, only a few miles distant.

'Tara.' It has a majestic ring to it. What do I know of it?

'The harp that once through Tara's halls
The soul of music shred,
Now hangs as mute on Tara's walls
As I that soul were fled.
So sleeps the pride of former days,
So glory's thrill is o'er,
And hearts, that once beat high for praise,
Now feel that pulse no more'

Tara was the High Place of Kings, royal residence of the monarchs for nearly 2000 years before the coming of Christianity. It was the seat of the Ard Ri, or High Kings from the time of Cormac MacArt in the third century to the reign of King Dermot, when Tara was abandoned in A.D.565.

Long ago, five broad ways led to the Hill but now there is nothing but the wind in the grass and the sheep; quietly munching their way to Valhalla or wherever their heaven is. I look at them; they personify contentment, not knowing their eventual fate and think of the poem by Robert Burns as his plough unearths the nest of a field mouse...
'but thou art blessed compared wi' me,
The present only toucheth thee'

Will humans, in their complexity, ever attain contentment?
Perhaps God created this discontent deliberately. Without it, would we still be living in caves and clad in animal skins! Who knows?

There is something about this island that induces this state of mind and especially so around Tara.

I must push on. I am anxious to get to the 'Bronte's homeland.

It is 1pm and the rain has stopped. The surrounding countryside with its rich pastures and fields of golden corn swaying in gentle waves as the warm summer breeze passes over them presents a heavenly sight. The old gods and kings chose their site well.

XXXVII

The way to Dundalk can be taken without touching the main roads. The winding country lanes, though they may seem interminably long, are still preferable to the mindless main roads.

In the distance can be seen the Mountains of Mourne, adding additional splendour to the countryside. I hear John McCormack, Ireland's golden voiced tenor, singing, as no one else in the world can, its refrain.

Once again, I ponder:
Is there any other country where at every turn and quarter there is something romantic and haunting to greet you?

As one nears them, the varying patterns of colours can be seen more clearly. Overhead, the white cotton balls of cloud in the clear blue sky hang over them as they stand so proud and majestic, almost like a great, benign giant, guarding his domain.

I come to Slane; only a tiny village but like everywhere else in this country there is something to halt you. I am directed to the Hill of Slane, where St. Patrick had lit a Paschal fire on Easter Eve in 433AD in defiance of the Druids who were preparing a great Pagan festival at Tara.

I was reminded that the film, 'Captain Boycott' was shot around Slane.

I was heading for Dundalk but before that I came to the attractive little market town of Ardee on the River Dee. In the past, this was often used as a mustering point for English forces before they attacked Ulster.
There are two castles in the town; the 13th century Ardee Castle with its square keep, now a museum and gift shop, and Hatches Castle (now a private house) in Market Street which also dates from the 13th century.

Ardee stands at the northern boundary of the Pale, the area controlled by the English since the days of Henry 11.

We get the expression, 'beyond the Pale' as something outside the boundaries of civilized society.

It was here, at Ardee that the famed Cuchalainn, Champion of Ulster, gave battle to his foster-brother, Ferdia, the champion of the South.

XXXVIII

And thus, I came to Dundalk. As might be expected on a Saturday afternoon it is throng. Maybe it is because of its little narrow streets and general tightly contained buildings that the number of cars seem to swamp the town, but they do! They appear to 'infest' the streets, obscuring the shop fronts and other buildings.

I was last here in 1992. In 2009 it is not much different; perhaps more affluent, as is all Ireland since it joined the EU. But compared with the Dundalk pre-war … 'a different world'.

I quote Morton:
'Everything that can happen in an Irish market town was happening in Dundalk. The wide central place before the Town Hall was packed with people; and I have never seen so many women taking part in an Irish market day. Carts were piled up in the main street. Calves mooed under string nets. Pigs squealed and grunted. Geese hissed and gobbled. On trestles before the Town Hall were set out all sorts of things from silk stockings to tin buckets. Strange and alien in this typical Irish crowd was one of those Orientals who hopelessly peddle rugs and bits of bright cloth round the world. He was a young fellow and he spoke rather bad English. He told me that he was born near Calcutta:
'How do you get on in Ireland? How do they treat you? Where do you live?'
'The Irish…good peoples', he said… 'kind peoples. They let me sleep in stables and they give food. I know Scotland too. Good people there too, far north in the mountains but in the south, not so good. They think you come to steal. But the Irish kind good peoples, share food with you. Oh, very nice and very kind…'

I had an indifferent lunch in a respectable restaurant and again I was reminded of HV Morton's visit all those years ago.

He is nonplussed how a country that grows such quality foodstuffs; such butter, such fresh eggs and bacon and such meat, and such vegetables, straight from a garden, how it becomes so unpleasant and often uneatable after it has passed through the kitchen.

I cannot use strong words like that but 'indifferent' is still no accolade.

Quite a different picture from today.

Dundalk is the county town of Louth. It is a busy manufacturing town sitting at the head of Dundalk Bay. In times past it was a fortress guarding the pass through the mountains to the province of Ulster.

It was the scene of battles involving Vikings, Anglo-Normans and English, all fighting to command this strategic site. There is little left to remind us of these epic times now, and since the 18th century peace has reigned.

Unlike other Irish towns, the Civic buildings erected when the town had prospered, did not reflect Irish traditional architecture. Instead, The Courthouse was modelled on the Temple of Theseus in Athens. There is an inscription beneath the statue of the 'Maid of Eireann' on the plaza outside, commemorating the Fenian uprising of 1798.

XXXIX

I head up the N1 to Newry. I see a sign to Warren-Point. I recall the recent IRA bombing outrage but on a more pleasant note remember its other connections with the Brontes, (or Bruntys, Brantys, Prumtys. Spellings were not important then.)

Way back, in the early18th century, the great grandfather of Patrick Bronte, the father of the three famous sisters, had a small farm near Newry. He was a cattle-dealer and regularly sailed from Warren Point to Liverpool to buy and sell cattle. When he, a Protestant, married a flame-haired Catholic beauty named Alice McClory, against family opposition they spent their honeymoon here.

The story goes that on returning to Warren Point, a stowaway in the form of a dirty, bedraggled little boy, wrapped in rags, with dark skin and tousled black hair, thought to be a gypsy, was found. Great consternation was caused and only after persistence from Mrs Brunty did they eventually agree to let her take him home with them. He was given the name of Welsh and accepted as one of the family. Mr Brunty came to love the boy even more than his own children...

It does not require much imagination to see here the link with Emily Bronte's 'Wuthering Heights'! We do know that Hugh Brunty was renowned locally as a story-teller and no doubt this story was passed down to Patrick who, most likely told it to his own daughters.

The Bruntys had been long resident in Ireland when Patrick won a sizership to Cambridge University as his first step to entering 'the church'.

Either it was because they couldn't understand his broad Irish vogue or (more likely) a deliberate mistake to create a new persona that he became 'Bronte'.

It is no coincidence that his favourite hero was Lord Nelson of Bronte; a title given to him by the Italians. The Bruntys now became, Brontes. I look forward to discovering Bronte Land.

I had been told to look out for the sign to Carlingford. I saw it...
'Beautiful, mediaeval. Carlingford'

Carlinford lies on the other side of the Cooloey Peninsula and I take the R72 that brings me there.

The first view of Carlingford is surprising. Suddenly, I see a picturesque old village dotted with ruined old castles, standing on the edge of a beautiful Lough. Behind it, its outline lying like a sleeping giant is a huge, steep rising mountain.

The village itself, with its narrow alleyways and twisting and winding streets, has a distinctly French provincial flavour. An old lady stands in the doorway of her 15th century old shop.

It is an ancient place now taken over by the National Heritage. Here, it is said, St. Patrick first landed. The Vikings came some centuries later but the oldest survival from the past is King John's Castle down by the water's edge. With the walls rising some seventy feet it is the largest Norman castle in the country. It was built about 1210 and King John is said to have stayed there.

Further history of the town can be explored in the Holy Trinity Heritage Centre, housed in a medieaval church.

In summer the town is busy with numerous festivals of one kind and another.

This morning, several young men who had been staying here set off on their bicycles to explore the surrounding Mountains of Mourne that rise steeply in an awe inspiring mass of greens and browns to meet the blue sky above.
I thought also, of the two young men I had seen a short way down the coast road in 1992. They were not in cycling shorts and Tee shirts, preparing for a day's run in the countryside but dressed, obscenely, in

heavy camouflaged bullet-proof clothing. They were manning the Check-Point on the border.

My landlady, an informant on esoteric history, informed me that King John stayed here for a night and a day and never did anything more interesting or destructive than play cards. Although I am a student of history, I never had heard of this event. I thanked her for this exclusive piece of Anglo-Irish relationship. I was pleased to think he had time for such innocuous pleasure when he had Robin Hood to contend with.

On this Sunday morning in 2009, the town was quiet; such a contrast to the hurley-burley of the tourist spots in the Republic. Although there are a collection of ruined old castles, the two main ones are: King John's, a ruin overlooking the Lough and a large Keep in the town. A wall, parts of which are standing, once surrounded the town.

As might be expected, the ancient town is full of legends.
One is that a volcanic eruption threw the original town into a Lough. The giant Finn Mcool, whose profile you see in the mountains outline, lies up there, overlooking the town. This giant, the same one of Giant's Causeway fame, seems to be the main folk-legend of Ireland. Legend has it that Lough Neagh, the largest lake in the British Isles was formed when he plucked out the land, leaving the great lake and hurled it into the middle of the Irish Sea and creating the Isle of Man.

Is it a coincidence that the island is the same shape and size of Lough Neagh?

I was disappointed that nowhere did I hear tales of fairies or leprechauns or any other folk-lore. When I spoke to one young Irishman about this apparent lack of interest, he smiled and said, that such tales were only told to non-Irish as a 'leg-pull'.

Whatever truth there may be in that, I am sorry that to the young generation of Ireland they now mean nothing, I hope he is wrong.

XL

In 1992 crossing the border was surprising in the fact that I was not aware it had been crossed! It is true there was a flimsy-looking brown shed with a dirty-looking broken pane of glass, bearing sadly, a notice board which said, 'CUSTOMS'. It appeared empty but when you approached it, a bored face nodded you through, back to the United Kingdom.

At Newry, things were different. The place seemed empty, both of people and traffic. As I entered the town, a young soldier, looking no more than eighteen, walked across the road, rifle at the ready, obviously alert for any sign of trouble. Up the street opposite were several more armed soldiers, spaced on either side of the road to cover each other.

I was excited to find myself in 'Bronte Land'. The novels and the tragic story of the family have fascinated me for years. Now here I was in the land where their roots were. The A25 is a good road that takes you to Rathfriland. In this area of Rathfriland, Ballyrooney, Bainbridge and Loughbrickland, is where Patrick spent his first twenty six years. Northern Ireland has recognised its interest by putting up signs pointing to 'The Bronte Homeland'.

Rahfriland was quiet and empty but a lady I sought information from, informed me she too was interested in the 'Bronte story' and gave me directions to the cabin where Patrick was born, also the school at which he taught until his departure for Cambridge.

After what seemed many miles on circuitous, wanderings uphill and down vale I came to Drumballyrooney Church. Here, a notice told me that at this church, which also served as a school, Patrick first taught. Some of the information she forwarded was at odds with other generally accepted views. She omitted to tell me that Patrick left this school under a cloud! We have been given to understand that he was a red-blooded, vigorous young man and to learn that he became involved with a girl pupil at the school is quite believable. He was moved to another school where he was noted for his modern, innovative ideas on education. He held evening classes for adults and organised a gymnasium.

The notice board said he returned to Ireland to preach after his ordination in England, although the truth is, he never returned.
However, he sent money to his mother all her life until her death...

In his book, 'The Road To Haworth', John Cannon relates in detail the saga of the Bruntys in Ireland.

XLI

Armagh has come to be known as the Irish Canterbury. It was here that St. Patrick built his cathedral and founded his school.

Armagh boasts two cathedrals. The Catholic one has twin towers and can be seen from either end of the town, from whichever way you enter.

The Protestant one is less obvious and less flamboyant.

The Catholic Cathedral has a remarkable story. It was erected to 'The Glory of God' and 'The Honour of Ireland' by Catholics from every part of the world. It took thirty years to build.

The Book of Armagh was written in the monastery in 807 AD. It is a copy of the New Testament in Latin. The school of Armagh that grew up beside the monastery was one of the most celebrated in Ireland in the 6th century. It opened its doors to scholars from every part of Europe.

One part of the city was called Trian-Saxon from the number of Saxons that lived there.

When the Norman invaders wrecked the ancient Gaelic civilisation there were 3000 scholars in residence receiving knowledge which Ireland alone had saved from the wreck of the Western world.

In 1992, when I was last here, there was a strong military presence. Huge walls of barbed wire surrounded the barracks and army HQ. In the streets, armed soldiers, rifles at the ready, moved cautiously and warily, ever alert for trouble.

I leave Armagh and am soon in the heart of Tyrone. It is one of the most beautiful of the inland counties. It is a farming county and is the least populated in Ulster. I am anxious to visit the 'Ulster-American' Folk-Lore Park, built to show the links between Ulster and America.

The Theme Park tells the story of the great waves of emigration from Ulster during the 18th and 19th centuries. In the Old World area of the park are thatched craftsmen's cottages, a forge and a school house. There are regular demonstrations of old skills such as candle-making, fish salting and horse-shoeing. There is the re-creation of an Ulster main street in 1900.

In the New World section there are log houses, a Pennsylvania farmstead, a covered wagon and a full-scale replica of an emigrant ship.

The History Park, opened some years ago, is some six or seven miles NW of Omagh. There are some large modern buildings that one may imagine to be a new style Roman Catholic Church and a large Visitors Centre. There is a guided tour through the buildings that tell us the history of life in Ireland over the last 5000 years.

There are several large burial chambers, huts of the Stone Age, the Bronze Age, Lake Dwellers, Monastic Cells, and churches, a refuge tower, and a Motte and Bailey like castle of early Norman times.

My time is now running out and I have to be in Larne by 11.30.am tomorrow. Now at 5.30pm I am still in the middle of Ireland; no place booked to stay the night and quite a few miles yet to cover.

Fortunately, the roads are good and it did not take long to reach the outskirts of Belfast. Here again, in 1992 we met with the armed patrols. Traffic was being delayed as cars were stopped and scrutinised before being waved on.

I had noticed then, with some sorrow, the youthfulness of these young soldiers, with their faces daubed hideously with camouflaged war paint. If one did not know how deadly serious it all was, it could be seen as pathetic or even farcical.

The scene in 2009 is more peaceful and hopefully as time proceeds, so will those memories.

Regretfully, Belfast will have to wait but I am coming to Carrickfergus and I must find a place for tonight.

XLII

On Sunday night the town is deserted. It appears plague-stricken. There are lines of parked cars but no sign of a living soul.

Accommodation was not difficult to find. The hotel overlooking the harbour seemed quiet and empty but on entering the dining-room there was a sharp contrast.

The large room was full of diners. Waiters and waitresses in traditional black and white, darted about attending to every need, while concealed speakers blasted out the same aggressive, cacophony of discordant 'musak' as one meets in England.

If there is depression in N. Ireland, it is certainly 'not here' in this room.
I remember my history. Here in 1778, a ship disguised as a merchantman appeared off Carrckfergus. It was the notorious 'Ranger' commanded by that son of a Scottish gardener, Paul Jones. The crew of a fishing smack boarded her and Paul Jones, on learning that they were pilots, detained them. They told him that the ship he could see lying in Belfast Lough was the British Sloop-o-war, 'Drake' of twenty guns. Paul Jones then planned an attack that was to reverberate all over Britain, and, incidentally lead to the independence of Ireland.

Jones has left a detailed description of the fight. However, his plans went astray. His plan was to sneak up, disguised as a merchantman and expose her decks to his fire but a strong storm blew up and Jones abandoned his plan and made off to carry his daring and historic raid on Whitehaven. He burnt the shipping in this port and a few hours after landed at St. Mary's Isle, Kirkcudbright, with the idea of capturing the Earl of Selkirk.

On the 24th April he was again off Carrickfergus, where he saw The Drake moving out of Belfast Lough. By now, news of his escapade at Whitehaven had spread and the Drake was under orders to find him.

The Drake's boat was sent out to reconnoitre the Ranger. When the ship's officer boarded the privateer he was at once made prisoner. The Drake was accompanied by five smaller vessels full of Belfast folk who wanted to see a naval battle. As the Drake approached and the Ranger manoeuvred for position, alarm smoke appeared on both sides of the channel, and the sightseers put back.

The Drake came within hail and hoisted the Union Jack. The Ranger ran up the American Stars. In a few moments the first broadside broke from the side of the Ranger and swept the Drake. The two ships then engaged in battle for over an hour. The Drake then called for quarter, being badly hit.

This was America's first naval victory, won in the sight of thousands of Belfast people who clearly demonstrated their sympathy with the new U.S.A. although great alarm was caused throughout Britain and militia camps sprang up all over the country.

The Irish, Protestant and Catholic demanded that as England could not defend them, in the event of war they should be allowed to organise a volunteer force similar to the Militia that was training all over England.

Belfast led the way. 40,000 men were enlisted within a year. They were armed and put in uniform.

In return for this gesture, some of the restrictions on Catholics were lifted, and also that of trade and Irish exports and in 1782 certain of the penal laws were lifted.

This led to further emancipation. Parliamentary independence was granted... 'Home Rule!'

An Irish Parliament sat in Dublin.

Carrickfergus is the ancient capital of Ulster. It is impressive with its magnificent castle on a rock - a square Norman Keep and a great wall commanding Belfast Lough.

The castle is now an 'Ancient Monument' and has been restored to make it one of the great attractions of N. Ireland tourism.

It is said to have been built in the wildest days of Irish history, when, in the reign of Henry 11, Anglo-Welsh adventurers, led by one of their tempestuous kind, - a John De Courcy, a penniless adventurer who had heard the legend that Ulster would be conquered by a pauper knight from a foreign country. He would be on a white horse bearing birds upon his shield. The prophecy was that Ulster would wade in blood. De Courcey made himself, as much as he could like the legend.

With a small, well armed band of 320 knights and Welsh archers he set out to conquer Ulster.

Downpatrick was attacked and slaughter and pillage was the order of the day. De Courcey fought for years to conquer Ulster, consolidating any victory by building a castle like Carrick.

Eventually, his enemies intrigued against him and procured his arrest as a traitor. An interesting story is told how on a Good Friday his servants came upon him, kneeling, unarmed and in sackcloth doing penance in the cathedral.

When he saw he was to be attacked he seized the nearest weapon, a huge wooden cross on a grave and dashed out the brains of thirteen men before he was overpowered. Strangely, he was not killed and his end is a mystery.

Carrickfergus as a tourist centre has lots to offer. The castle now houses the Cavalry Regimental Museum with its magnificent array of weapons and armour and life-size figures. There are costumed guides and a video presentation provides a fascinating insight into the castle's history.

There is also 'The Knight Ride', Ireland's only themed mono-rail which transports passengers through one thousand years of the town's history, like the Yorvik Centre in York, complete with all the contemporary sounds and smells of the time.

For students of literature, the town boasts some eminent figures. The Restoration playwright William Congreve grew up here in the castle where his father was a soldier. Jonathan Swift's first clerical appointment was at Kilroot, just outside the town, where he wrote, 'the Tale of a Tub'. More recently, Louis MacNeice, (1907-63) the poet, spent a despondent childhood which he recalled in his uncomplimentary poem, 'Carrickfergus'.

His father was the Minister at the church of St. Nicholas, originally built by De Courcey in 1205.

Of especial interest to American visitors is the 'Andrew Jackson' cottage. It was from Carrickfergus that the parents of the seventh US President set sail in 1765 for the American colonies.

In the gardens of the Andrew Jackson Centre is the 'US Rangers Centre.' It tells the story of this elite combat unit whose first unit was formed at Carrickfergus in 1942. The exhibition contains uniforms, vintage radio equipment, documents and photographs.

Of more contemporary interest is a visit to, 'Flame', the Gasworks Museum of Ireland.

The works were built in 1855 to produce gas for the town's streets; this is the only coal-fired gasworks in Ireland.

XLIII

Belfast lies some nineteen miles north of Downpatrick on the A24, and halfway there I come to the pleasant little market town of Ballynahinch with its façade of fine little shops. It is Saturday, market day and bustling. Like so many of the little towns and villages I have passed through, I think, 'I could live here.'

All these quaint little places seem to have some item of interest. Ballynahinch has a castle, which is now a luxury hotel but it was once a fine house built by a family named Martin. The most famous of this family was 'Humanity Martin.' He became the founder of the RSPCA.
In the 1950s, the famous Indian cricketer, Ranjitsinghi or 'Ranji' as he was known, bought it.

I have often wondered why so many Irish towns are pre-fixed with 'Bally.'
'It simply means, 'Township,' I was told.

Further north I come to Newtownards. It presents a different picture to Ballynahinch.

This is a busy manufacturing town standing near the Northern tip of Strangford Lough and although the town is over 700 years old there is nothing ancient left except the ruins of a Dominican Priory.

A mile or so outside the town is Scrabo Park in which stands Scrabo Tower, built in 1857 as a memorial to the Marquis of Londonderry for his relief efforts during the great famine.

A couple of miles north is 'The Somme Heritage Centre'. This recalls the part played by the Irish and Ulster Divisions in the most horrific of battles in the First World War.

The Battle of the Somme lasted for five months. When the German forces eventually receded, the British forces had won a few miles of shell-pocked mud at the cost of 600,000 lives.

At the centre here, staff in battle-dress recount the terrible story and the re-created front-line trenches re-live and underline the horror.

Nearby is 'The Ark'. This is Ireland's first rare breed farm and is home to over eighty rare species of cattle, pig, sheep, goats, ponies, poultry and llama, all in forty acres of countryside. There is also an educational/activity centre, farm shop, picnic site, play areas and a tea garden.
Ireland is learning its 'Tourist Trade' well.

After leaving Newtownards and seeing Holywood, which, in my haste, I read 'Hollywood', I couldn't resist to urge to visit the Irish one, having only recently been in the other one.

It is an attractive little residential town standing on Belfast Lough. There are some fine sandy beaches and long coastal walks. The major visitor attraction is the Ulster Folk and Transport Museum, one of the best museums in the country.

There is an 'Open Air' part of the complex which shows Ulster in 1910, with a farm, using the methods and equipment of a bygone age.

Bangor, my next stop, is to Belfast what Blackpool is to Burnley and the Lancashire Mill Towns. It serves as its lung.

Its heyday was in Victorian times and the town still retains many of its Victorian features. Its proximity to Belfast leaves it open to a continual flow of day-trippers and like Blackpool has its complement of shops and amusement centres. Ballyholme Bay is a splendid beach with its splendid Victorian type 'Ward Park' and its one day open market.

In the outbuildings of Bangor Castle is the North Down Heritage Centre displaying the archaeology, early Christian history and Natural History of the area. Of interest to the epicurean is the superior type restaurant, while Pickie Park is a must for the kids.

It was while I was in Carrickfergus, I saw an old film on TV; it was, 'Mutiny On The Bounty' with those great Hollywood stars, Charles Laughton, Clark Gable and Franchot Tone.

It was the last name that caught my attention... 'Tone'.
I did some hasty research and sure enough found that the actor was a direct descendant of the 'Wolfe Tone' who had played such an important part in Irish history.

Wolfe Tone was the founder of the United Irishmen. It embraced both Protestant and Catholic alike and sought only the welfare of Ireland. It became a great secret society and the means to hatching a rebellion.

With a name like Franchot I had assumed he was of French descent but I learned that Wolfe went to France, where he ended his days.

XLIV

Since the American colonies declared their independence, Ulster has contributed nearly half of their Presidents! Such was the emigration to the American colonies from Ulster that at the declaration of independence, one sixth of the population was of Ulster descent!

It is still fiercely loyal to the crown. The defiance of the I.R.A. is shown by the flagrant display from nearly every window of Union Jacks and the Ulster flags, a red cross on a white background. The pavement edges are painted red and white, while on walls, in letters six feet high, are slogans like 'God Save The Queen'.

It is a pity that such a division should seem necessary but both sides are implacable in their stand.

This is such a beautiful little island, with its generous open-hearted people but the division is so deeply rooted in religion and politics that one wonders, will there ever be a solution?
Larne lies only a few miles further along the coast. The road runs past rows of poor working-class terraced houses. I remember, in 1992 when 'the troubles' were still on how it brought a lump to the throat to see how these ordinary people gave their response to the IRA and its terrorism.

It is a pity that such a terrible conflict between, of all things …Christians, should have arisen. The roots go deep and are never ending. It is not merely religion. It is politics, economics, nationalism, injustice, corruption, avenge and revenge. Put them all together and boil over the last thousand years and you have Ireland. Waiting for the next Messiah to sort things out?

The A2 takes me to Larne on the last stage of my journey. This is the shortest sea route to the mainland of England and Scotland. Had no time to linger when I arrived but now, with a few hours to spare, am anxious to see more of it.

On a clear day the Scottish coast is plainly visible. The Curran is a long gravel spit curving outwards from the town. It is a 'must' for archaeologists and many thousands of flints, arrowheads and tools have been found; evidence that this was one of the first parts of Ireland to be inhabited.

During the period of mass emigration to the New World, Larne was one of the major embarkation points for emigrants.

In Curran Park I found a striking bronze statue depicting a family about to leave their homeland.

At the southern tip of the Curran stand the ruins of Oldfield Castle, originally a Viking foundation but rebuilt in stone in the 13th century. It is now surrounded by an industrial park.

There is an interesting memorial to the man who was the driving force behind the establishment of shipping routes from Larne to Scotland and the Americas.

James Chaime, a County Antrim MP for whom, in 1888 the Round Tower, modelled on the lines of an ancient Irish round tower was built, so loved watching the passing ships that he stipulated the manner of his burial. He was to be interred in an upright position in a private enclosure overlooking the harbour so that he could still watch the passing ships.

Larne Borough Council has taken over Carfunnock Country Park with its 500 acres of woodland, gardens and walking trails, and beach and added a visitor centre, 9 hole golf course,   adventure playground, miniature railway and a maze of hornbeams in the shape of Northern Ireland.

The estate was once the home of Sir Thomas and Lady Dixon and many of its original features still remain, including the walled garden, the ice house and the lime kilns.

And so I leave Ireland once more, as ever, with mixed feelings.

My romantic Ireland, if it ever existed, is now sadly gone but a more realistic Ireland is here to entrance everyone with its beauty, its history and above all, its people.

Since the writing of this travelogue, Ireland has suffered a tragic economic collapse. It seems Ireland is once again in for dramatic changes but as before ... it will weather them!

EXTRA INFORMATION

More about Ireland (At a glance)

ACT OF UNION (1800)
Simultaneous acts passed in the parliaments of Dublin and London establishing the UK of Great Britain with Ireland.
Tourism giving it a new lease of life.

ADAMS Gerry b. 1948
Republican activist and politician. Sinn Fein's President - 1983

AHERN Bertie b. 1951
Fianna Fail statesman, Prime Minister - 1997.

ANGLO-IRISH AGREEMENT .1985
Agreement signed by Margaret Thatcher and Irish Taoiseach, Garret Fitzgerald. Seen as being crucial to laying the foundations for the peace protest of the 1990's.

APPRENTICE BOYS(1814)
Protestant political grouping, named after the 13 apprentices who shut the gates of Derry against an approaching Catholic army in 1688.

ARAN ISLES
Island group in Galway Bay. Irish cultural geography. JM Synge's 'The Aran Islands,' (1907) to Andrew McNeillie's, 'An Aran Keening'(2001)
One of the last outposts of traditional Irish Gaelic culture.

BECKETT Samuel (1906-1989)
Dublin born playwright and novelist. Winner of the Nobel Prize for literature in 1969.
Lived most of his life in France. Active in French Resistance until 1942, when he was betrayed to the Gestapo. Escaped and moved to south of France where he worked on a farm.
His most famous play, 'En Attendant Godot'. ('Waiting for Godo')

BEHAN Brendan (1923-64)
Dublin born writer. Best known works are: 'The Hostage'and 'The Quare Fellow'. Joined the IRA at an early age and arrested in Liverpool in 1939 for possession of fire-arms. Alcoholic addiction led to his death in 1964.

BELFAST

Ireland's pre-eminent industrial city. Population 475000. Since 1921 the capital of Northern Ireland. The rise of industrialism through the 18th century brought immigrants flooding in from Catholic Ireland. Determinedly defining themselves against these incomers, the city's tradesmen and skilled labourers made militant Protestantism and Loyalism the twin pillars of their status.

BLACK AND TANS (1920-1921)

Auxiliary police force working in Ireland. Irish police resigned in large numbers after World War 1 rather than face the rising Irish nationalism led by the IRA. The British government hired replacements, often unemployed ex service men. Lack of equipment meant army jackets or trousers were utilised alongside the police black. Hence the nick-name derived from a hound pack in Tipperary. Their ruthlessness and often illegal methods of retaliation against terrorists included brutal interrogation and house burning. They were disbanded in 1921.

BLARNEY CASTLE (1446)

Semi-ruined 15th century castle 6 miles NW of Cork. The fame of the place depends upon its mythical powers of the famous Blarney Stone. The stone is reputed to confer the gift of eloquence on anyone who kisses it.

BLOODY SUNDAY (1972)

Name given to the killing of 14 people by British Forces on Sunday 30th January 1972. An illegal civil rights demonstration went ahead despite being banned. Members of the Parachute Regiment opened fire on the protesters, shooting 13 on the spot. Many of the injured died later.

CARRIKFERGUS CASTLE 1180 AD

The castle is one of the best-preserved in Ireland. It remained an English stronghold when William111 conquered James 11 in 1689.

SIR ROGER CASEMENT 1864-1916. Knighted 1911.

British diplomat and Irish patriot.
Became disenchanted with British Colonial Rule.
Joined the 'Irish Volunteers'. Arrested while trying to import arms on the eve of the Easter Rising. Sentenced to death. Hanged at Wandsworth Prison-1916.

CROMWELL Oliver (1599-1658)
The Catholic Confederation had allied itself with the English Royalists and Ireland was now seen as a major threat. In 1649 Cromwell arrived in Ireland and attacked the rebel strongholds of Drogheda and Wexford, massacring the defenders - most of whom were English Royalists.
Cromwell saw these ruthless victories as a just revenge ordered by God for the massacre of Protestants in 1641.
He outlawed Catholic worship and that all Catholic lands east of the River Shannon should be seized and distributed amongst his troops. Only 22% of Ireland was left in Catholic ownership.
By 1649 Cromwell was commander-in-chief and Lord Lieutenant of Ireland.

De VALERA Eamon (1882-1975)
Statesman; President of executive council of the Irish Free State. (1923-37) Taoiseach (1937 -1948 -1951 - 1954 -1957 -1959)
Born in Brooklyn of Spanish-Irish parentage, De Valera was brought up by relatives in County Limerick and completing his education at University College, Dublin became a maths teacher. A member of the Gaelic League from 1908 and a volunteer from 1913. He had a good 'Rising', being the last commander to surrender in 1916. Sentenced to death, he was reprieved on the intervention of the US consul. Released from gaol 1917, he was rearrested the following year, accused of plotting with Germany but was sprung from prison and became President of the first D'ail Eireann between 1919 -20.
Having, it was said, manoeuvred Michael Collins and Arthur Griffith into signing the Anglo-Irish Treaty, de Valera rejected its terms, leading an opposition that would finally flare up into civil war. When the pro-Treaty faction won, de Valera was imprisoned for a time with other Republican leaders. He emerged to re enter constitutional politics, resigning his leadership of abstentionist Sinn Fein, in 1926. Prime Minister from 1923 (his Constitution of 1937 changed the title to Taioseach) He would dominate politics in the Free State for the next 40 years.

DEVLIN Bernadette (born 1947)
Republican Socialist Activist and politician. Played a prominent part in the Civil Rights Movement to gain equal rights for Catholics, particularly in the Battle of the Bogside, 1969. She was elected MP for Mid -Ulster, 1969 and was renowned for hitting the Home Secretary in the House of Commons. Bernadette and her husband survived a loyalist assassination attempt in which they were both badly injured.

The DIASPORA 1780

After the introduction of the Penal Laws and during the Great Famine, large numbers of Irish people left Ireland to form new lives in English speaking countries like the USA, the UK, Canada, Australia and New-Zealand, as well as to Argentina which has the largest non-English speaking Irish community in the world.

The negative version of the Diaspora began with the transportation of Irish convicts to Australia in 1780. These convicts had previously been transported to the American colonies but the War of Independence stopped that.

During the famine it is said that some Irish feigned crime in order to get free transport to Australia. By 1861 the Irish community made up 20% of the Australian population. In 1822 the British Parliament financed an emigration plan to Canada in order to increase the number of settlers available to defend Canada against the USA.

DUBLIN

Capital of the Irish Republic. 1 million inhabitants. (1/5th of all Ireland).

Founded in 841AD by the Vikings. Conquered by Anglo-Normans in 1204.

By mid 15th C. English were passing laws to exclude the Irish from trading.

The Act of Union -1800 ended Dublin as a political centre.

Dublin's middle-class Catholics began to see their disenfranchisement, not just in religious terms but in national terms.

In 1849 49% of Dubliners lived in single room accommodation.

By 1914 the figure was 25%.

The 1916 Easter Rising was held in horror by the majority of Dubliners.

Dublin is now as well-known for its drug problem as for its famous Georgian architecture.

FENIAN BROTHERHOOD

Revolutionary organisation founded on St. Patrick's Day, 1858.

Set out to establish an independent non-sectarian Ireland.

FENIAN MOVEMENT

Wider political movement that grew up around activities of Fenians

Fenian Rising. 1867

Political rebellion. The end of the American Civil War in 1865 with the resulting demobilisation of large numbers of Irish American soldiers, trained and battle-seasoned presented an opportunity for Fenianism in the old country but the leading figures were rounded up and it was squashed.

FIANNA FAIL 1926
Founded by De Valera- aim was an independent Irish Speaking
United Ireland by peaceful means. Opposed by N. Ireland Protestants and
the British State.

FINE GAEL 1933
Political party brought together three political parties in hopes of mounting
a coherent opposition.

FLIGHT of the EARLS (1607)
After his defeat at Kinsale and following his surrender at Melifont in1603,
O'Neil had been forced to relinquish his title and took that of The Earl of
Tyrone. With O' Donnell, signed the Treaty of Melifont with James 1 of
England. Fled to France. Rumours of a rebellion were spread and they were
summoned back to London. Finding the English rule unacceptable they
boarded a French ship from Rathmullen, together with their family and
followers and set off for Spain . Fierce storms forced the ship into France and
they decided to travel instead to Rome. The government declared their flight
treasonable and confiscated their lands.

GOOD FRIDAY AGREEMENT 1998
Political settlement reached on 10th April 1998 which allowed for an all-party
Assembly for the government of N. Ireland.

GUINNESS 1799
National beer of Ireland. Produced by the Guinness family since 1799. It is
sold in 120 countries.

HAUGHEY Charles (1925-2006)
Famous Fail politician. Taoiseeach 1979-81

HEANEY Seamus b 1939
Ireland's greatest English language poet. His first collection was 'Death of a
Naturalist' 1996.
In 1995 awarded the Nobel Prize for literature.

HEDGE SCHOOLS 1702 -1719
Schools established following the introduction of Penal Laws in 1702 and
1719. Irish Catholics set up institutions when the teaching of Catholic
religion was banned, illegal under English law. The lessons were paid for by

parents and were held by masters in places that were considered safe. In 1826 403,000 children were being taught the three 'R's and religion in Hedge Schools.

The National School System was set up in 1831. It provided free schooling but the use of the Irish language was prohibited.

HENRY V111 1491-1547
1537 Irish Parliament declared Henry, King of Ireland. Property confiscation from rebels and monasteries helped unify Irish opposition to English rule. In the latter part of the reign property was awarded to lords who renounced papal authority, but the process was erratic and arbitrary.

HOME RULE 1840s.
Dominant Irish political issue from the late nineteenth century and the first half of the twentieth century, emerging first in the 1840s from Daniel O'Connor and the Young Ireland Movement. Home rule came to the fore in the 1880s under pressure from Charles Stewart Parnell, capitalising on the reforming inclination of William Gladstone's Liberal government and the political machinations at Westminster, where Irish supporters played a vital role in the power struggle between Tories and Liberals.

World War 1 suspended the issue and led to an outbreak of violent sectarianism during and after the war.

Settlement ultimately created an independent Southern Ireland while Ulster was retained by Britain.

Following the great famine of the 1840's, ordinary Irish people became more interested in more radical methods of reform.

The Fenian Movement was founded in 1858, with the intent to exploit a moment when Britain was engaged in a major war elsewhere.

The Fenian uprising in 1865 and 1867 sustained the tradition of armed rebellion in pursuit of independence.

The disastrous winter of 1878-79 revived fears of another famine. It propelled land reform to the forefront of Irish politics.

Charles Stewart Parnell was a Protestant land-owner. His strident pursuit of Irish independence characterised his reputation in parliament.

Under pressure from Parnell, Gladstone's government passed the Radical Land Act of 1881. It forced fair rents, prevented unfair evictions and allowed tenants to control sale or transfer of their leases.

The Franchise Act 1884 allowed half a million poorer Catholic new voters and allowed Parnell to manipulate Home Rule into being the central issue of the 1885 election. Conservatives feared the British Empire would break up.

Catholic supporters of Home Rule, (Nationalists) saw this as the only way forward. Ulster Presbyterians feared the inevitable Catholic domination of any Home Rule Settlement.

In 1890, Parnell was accused of adultery with Kitty O'Shea. The colossal spiritual power of the Catholic Church destroyed his career and split the Irish Party. Gladstone made Parnell's expulsion as leader of the Irish Party a condition of further support for Home Rule.

Parnell's death in 1891 extinguished the zeal which had driven the Home Rule movement.

HUNGER STRIKE 1881
In 1981 a group of republican prisoners in the H blocks of Long Clesh began a hunger-strike in demand for better conditions, led by Bobby Sands, who died and thus became a martyr.

IRISH CIVIL WAR 1922/3
War between former members of the IRA.

Following the Treaty establishing Home Rule and Arthur Griffith and Michael Collins as its leaders in December 1921, the IRA split between those who accepted the Treaty and those who opposed it.

The opposition was led by Eamon de Valera, president of Sinn Fein.

Collins found himself arming Catholics in Ulster to protect themselves while his authority was challenged by anti-Treaty Republicans. Fighting broke out and the anti-Treaty Republicans capitulated.

Collins then embarked on an Ireland-wide campaign against anti-Treaty Republicans. But Griffith's death and the assassination of Collins in 1922 led to an Emergency Powers Bill in 1922 under William Cosgrave until the IRA collapsed in 1923.

IRISH NATIONAL LIBERATION ARMY 1974
Formed by Armed Republican groups (IRA and Sinn Fein). Aim to create an Irish Republican Society.

JOYCE JAMES 1882 -1941
One of the most influential Irish novelists of the 20th century.
Works included:'Ulysses', 'Finnnegan's Wake', 'Portrait of the Artist as a Young Man,' and his short stories, 'Dubliners', as well as poetry and plays.

KEVIN OF GLENDALOUGH
Hermit who lived in a cave at Glendalough in County Wicklow.

STATUTES OF KILKENNY 1366
Statutes governing life in the medieval English colony.
English was the only language allowed to be spoken.
Only English traditional laws allowed to settle disputes.
No arms or horses for the Irish

KNOCK County Mayo.
Place of Pilgrimage. A Marian vision in 1879. The Virgin's appearance attested by no fewer than fifteen people. Knock has been an official pilgrimage site since 1930.

LUSITANIA 1915
British liner sunk on May 7th 1915 by a German submarine off the coast of Ireland. Nearly 1200 passengers drowned. The ship was carrying munitions.

LYNCH Jack (1917 – 1999)
Fianna Fail Politician...Taoiseach. 1966-73

McCORMACK John 1884 -1945
Irish Opera singer. The greatest lyric tenor of his time.

MUNSTER PLANTATION 1580s
Aggressive colonisation of land in Munster from 1580s onward.
Irish tenants evicted and English newcomers settled.

NORTHERN IRELAND
Under the Government of Ireland act of 1920 six of the Ulster Counties remained part of the UK while the rest of Ireland went on to gain dominion status under the terms of the Anglo-Irish Treaty of 1921.

OMAGH County Tyrone
Scene of 'Real IRA' bombing', 15th August1988. Twenty nine killed, many injured.

ORANGE ORDER (1795)
Militant Protestant Society. The heart of Ulster Loyalism.

ORANGEISM
Ideology of the Orange Order. Battle of the Boyne in 1690 hailed as the achievement of Protestant supremacy.

ORMONDE - DUKES OF
James Butler 1st Duke of Ormonde (1610 -1688)

Represented the Crown's interest during the Confederate War. Cromwell destroyed his forces in 1649. He joined the exiled court of James 11. After the Restoration he re-instated the Anglican Church in Ireland.

O'SHEA Kitty 1846-1921
Wife of Captain William O'Shea, a Home Rule MP. Had a long affair with the nationalist leader, Parnell, which led to his political downfall.
The case affected the course of Irish history. The scandal split the Home Rule party as well as removing its most capable leader, Parnell.

PAISLEY Ian b.1926
Clergyman and politician. Known as 'the voice of Loyalism'.
Austere and uncompromising for more than thirty years. Opposed Sunningdale Agreement of 1973, the Anglo-Irish agreement of 1985 and the 'Peace Protest'.

PARNELL James Stewart 1846-1891
Politician. Elected to Parliament in 1875 on a Home Rule ticket.
Accused of expressing sympathy for the 'Phoenix Park' murders. His affair with Kitty O'Shea in 1889 destroyed his political career.

PHOENIX PARK MURDERS 1882
Political assassinations of 6th May 1882 of Lord Frederick Cavendish, Irish Chief Secretary and his 'under Secretary' T.H. Burke.

PROTESTANT ASCENDANCY
Rule of Ireland by Protestants (ruling class)
Henry V111's attempt to install a Protestant land -owning class loyal to England.

PROVISIONAL IRA 1969
Revolutionary organisation dedicated to the overthrow of British rule through a sustained campaign of bombings and shootings in Ireland and Britain.

PROTESTANTISM
Reforming movement of Christianity which, in protest against the authority of the Catholic Church broke away to form separate denominations in the 16th century.

REPUBLIC OF IRELAND
A Free State fully independent of Britain and Commonwealth by an Act of

the Dail passed in 1949 De Valera's vision was of an idealised village Ireland. Protectionism and isolation meant that such a system was self-perpetuating: the 1950 years were years of stagnation. By 1957 unemployment had reached 80,000 and emigrants were streaming out of the country. The European Community reconstructed Irish agriculture as a modern business.

REPUBLIC OF IRELAND ACT (1948)
Legislation by which Ireland officially seceded from the British Commonwealth.

ROBINSON MARY (Born 1944)
Politician President of the Irish Republic (1990-1997)

SANDS BOBBY (1954-81)
Revolutionary and hunger-striker. Leader of IRA inmates in Long Clesh prison. First casualty of the hunger strike of 1981.

SHAW GEORGE BERNARD (1856 -1950)
Dublin born playwright.Won Nobel Prize for literature in 1925. Spent most of his adult life in England where he became the most successful dramatist of his day.
Plays include Pymalion, St.Joan, Arms and the Man, and John Bull. Socialist and pacifist.

STORMONT (1932)
Parliament building of Northern Ireland.

TARA
Prehistoric complex and semi-mythical seat of the Irish High Kings in County Meath. A burial site since the second millennium BC.

TITANIC (1912)
Built by Harland and Wolff in Belfast shipyards. World's largest ocean liner. While attempting to set a record for the trans-Atlantic crossing it struck an iceberg off Newfoundland and sunk within a few hours with the loss of 1490 lives.

Tone Theobald Wolfe (1763 -98)
Revolutionary. Born into a Protestant family and trained as a lawyer.

Believed in Irish independence from Britain. Became Secretary of The Catholic Committee. Forced into exile, first in America and then France. Captured before he could play any part in the 1798 uprising, he committed suicide while waiting under sentence of death.
An ancestor of Franchot Tone, the famous American movie star of 'Mutiny on the Bounty' and many others.

TRANSPORTATION (1789- 1868)
Transportation of convicted criminals to prisons in Australia.
Used as a means of disposing Irish dissidents. The 1798 rebellion increased the numbers between 1800 and 1805.

TRIMBLE David (b 1944)
Ulster Unionist politician. In 1990 elected MP for Upper Bann, remaining hostile to compromise with Republicans.
Became party leader in 1998. Compromise with the Republicans, making the Good Friday Peace agreement viable, winning the Nobel Peace Prize. He resigned on July 1st 2001 over the IRA failure to disarm.

THE TROUBLES (1960 -1994)
Period of sectarian warfare that broke out in Ulster in the late 1960s, continuing until the cease-fire in 1994. Sectarian troubles stretching back to 1610 Ulster Plantation and beyond.

U2
Ireland's most successful Rock Group. Formed in Dublin in 1977.

ULSTER DEFENCE ASSOCIATION (1971)
Loyalist Paramilitary Group set up with the aim of protecting Northern Ireland's Protestant communities.
Nationalists saw its main function as being intimidatory.
The Ulster Freedom Fighters (UFF) were responsible for a series of sectarian murders from the mid seventies to1994.

ULSTER PLANTATION of 1610
Part of the process of evicting Irish Catholic farming communities from their land in Ulster and imposing the settlement of English Protestant or Scottish Presbyterian landowners. This was followed by the Cromwellian Plantation of 1652 and the Williamite Plantation of 1693.
80% of Ireland's productive land had been transferred to ethnically and religiously distinct communities.
The vast bulk of Ireland's agrarian wealth had been transferred to non-

native landlords, causing catastrophic poverty among the indigenous population. A modern day, 'Ethnic Cleansing.'
The consequences helped to provoke the 1641 Rebellion, establish the Ulster Presbyterian communities and the polarisation of religious tribalism.

WARBECK Perkin (1474-1499)
Pretender to the English throne, claiming to be Richard 1V supposedly one of the 'little princes' said to have been murdered in the Tower of London by their uncle, Richard 111.
Arrived in Cork 1491 stating he was going to England to depose Henry V11. Found support from Ireland, Scotland and France. Invasion attempt in 1495 met with failure. Arrested by English forces and hanged, 1499.

WATERLOO Battle of (1815)
Climax of the Napoleonic Wars(16-18 June 1815).
Napoleon, Emperor of France, 1804. Abdicated 1814 but made a final bid for power in 1815. Faced Wellington and Prussian allies under Blucher at Waterloo. Weight of numbers carried the day and Napoleon was defeated.

WELLESLEY Arthur (1769-1852)
(1st DUKE OF WELLINGTON)
Soldier and statesman, British Prime Minister 1828-30-34. Opposed Catholic Emancipation.

WILDE OSCAR (1854-1900)
Irish novelist and playwright. Born in Dublin but moved to London to pursue his literary career. Well known as an extravert and a wit, he achieved great success with a number of comedies written for the stage, including 'Lady Windermere's Fan', (1892) 'The Importance of Being Ernest', 'An Ideal Husband' (1895)
In the same year took an unsuccessful libel action against the Marquis of Queensbury. Evidence produced during the counter charge led to a conviction for sodomy. Served two years in jail, disgraced and bankrupt. Died in poverty in Paris 1900.

YEATS William Butler(1865-1939)
Irish poet and dramatist. Awarded Nobel Prize for Literature in 1932. Born in Dublin but spent time in England and only began to appreciate his Irishness in his early twenties. Collaborated with Lady Gregory on the development of an Irish National Theatre, later, the Abbey Theatre. Served as a Senator in the government of the Irish Free State. Died near Monaco and his remains were later buried at Drumcliffe in County Sligo where his grandfather had been rector.

BIBLIOGRAPHY

Blacker,W and Wallace,R. *Formation of the Orange Order 1795 – 98*

Boylan,C. *Home Rule*, 1997, Abucus UK

J. Burgess Publications, *Dublin and Irish History*, 2000

Campbell,F. *Protestant Democracy in Ulster from Plantation to Partition*, 1991, Blackstaff Press

Colum, P. *The Road Round Ireland*, 1930, MacMillan

Corbridge, S.L.,*We go to Ireland*, 2001, Harrop

Fraser, A. *Our Chief of Men*, 1973, Panther

Green, A.S. *The Making of Ireland and its Undoing*, 1908, MacMillan

Gibbon, J. *Tramping through Ireland*, 1930, Methuen

Gwynne, S. *Ireland*, Harrop

Hodge, T. *Parnell and the Irish Question*, 1998, Longman

Lynd, R. *Ireland a Nation*, 1919, Grant Richards

MacAnnaidh, S. *Irish History*, 2001, Starfire

Morton, H.V. *In Search of Ireland*, 1930, Methuen

Catholic Emancipation in Ireland 1823-9, Greenwood Press

Sinn Fein and Socialism, 1991,Greenwood Press

INDEX

CPSIA information can be obtained at www.ICGtesting.com
Printed in the USA
BVOW061011310512

291483BV00001B/81/P

9 781907 728389